MEDICAL LIBRARY

P9-CFX-283

*Praise for*
# TRUE PARTNERSHIP

"The practice of partnership comes from your philosophy of partnership. *True Partnership* is a powerful tool for shaping your philosophy into a form that fosters partnership greatness."

—**Chip Bell**, author of *Customers As Partners*
and coauthor of *Dance Lessons: Six Steps to
Great Partnerships in Business and Life*

"I have seen too many times where a lack of collaboration between people becomes the root cause of business inefficiencies and loss of competitive advantage. Zaiss' book helps us understand why and how to change our attitudes and behaviors to form richer and more satisfying partnerships."

—**Russ Millholland**, Director of Human Resources,
Saint-Gobain Ceramics and Plastics

"Once again Carl has articulated a powerful vision for our relationships and delivers the principles and practices to accomplish it. Applying his model makes life more satisfying at work and at home."

—**Mark Siegfried**, Regional Sales Manager, Digital Island

"Powerful partnerships make for a good life. If you read this book it will make you a more conscious partner, and a more open, honest, creative and powerful human being."

—**Brad Blanton**, Ph.D., author of
*Radical Honesty* and *Practicing Radical Honesty*

"Yes this is a business book, but you will cheat yourself if you consider it as just another business book. Zaiss presents a viewpoint that is outside the norm of the traditional business book. It will provoke your mind. It will not gather dust."

—**JoAnn Dye**, Director of Training and Development,
Great American Insurance

"Don't miss the profound message of this book. *True Partnership* issues a quite challenge to discover the possibilities of every relationship, every encounter."

—**Jeff Wilson**, Senior Manager, Deloitte Consulting

"Caution! This book cannot be read just once. Each chapter is loaded with compelling insights that will show you how to take your relationships to the next level. Carl offers timeless principles that have both personal and professional applications. This book should be required reading in Corporate America."

—**Richard Basch**, Director of Training
and Development, A-TEK, Inc.

"These communication strategies are very simple, yet extremely powerful, and will make a profound difference in all of your personal and professional relationships. Live these concepts, share them with everyone you know, and reap the rewards of satisfying relationships."

—**Mary Stern**, President, Metro DC Chapter of
American Society of Training and Development

"In a fast-paced world, this insightful book is an excellent guide on how to take control and get beyond life's roadblocks and how to alter your relationships to achieve greater success."

—**Gary Decatur**, President, Choice Hotels of Canada

"In this increasingly wired, interconnected, networked world, the quality of our expanding relationships increases in importance. Zaiss' book lays out a way that anyone can improve the effectiveness—and consequently the value—of those relationships. The nature of relationships is changing and this book helps show you how you can change too."

—**Peter Leyden**, Knowledge Developer, Global Business Network
and coauthor of *The Long Boom: A Vision for the Coming Age
of Prosperity* and former managing editor of *Wired* magazine

"*True Partnership* uses a fresh approach to address the age-old organizational requirement for team building and leadership training. I found this book to be clear and full of common sense ideas adaptable to the everyday business environment."

—**Sue Richter**, National Vice President,
International Humanitarian Organization

"Carl Zaiss gives us a way of approaching relationships that pre-empts their breakdown and he empowers us with a surprisingly simple model for repairing relationships that are already strained. The outcome is partnership—a highly desirable state that is too rarely achieved in organizational life."

—**Ira Chaleff**, Chairman of the Board, Congressional
Management Foundation and author of *The Courageous
Follower: Standing Up To and For Our Leaders*

"Embrace Carl's message and transform your connection and communication with others. His authentic, creative writing approach reminds us that we are the source of true partnership in both individual and organizational effectiveness."

—**Annette Hurley**, Life Coach, Change Champion, and
Leader of Learning, Booz-Allen & Hamilton, Inc.

# TRUE PARTNERSHIP

MEDICAL LIBRARY
NORTH MEMORIAL HEALTH CARE
3300 OAKDALE AVENUE NORTH
ROBBINSDALE, MN 55422-2900

MEDICAL LIBRARY
NORTH MEMORIAL HEALTH CARE
3300 OAKDALE AVENUE NORTH
ROBBINSDALE, MN 55422-2900

# TRUE PARTNERSHIP

## REVOLUTIONARY THINKING ABOUT RELATING TO OTHERS

Carl Zaiss

MEDICAL LIBRARY
NORTH MEMORIAL HEALTH CARE
3300 OAKDALE AVENUE NORTH
ROBBINSDALE, MN 55422-2900

BK

BERRETT-KOEHLER PUBLISHERS, INC.
San Francisco

HD30.3
Z21t

Quotation from Joan Holmes, from her speech "Altering an Era," at the 1988 Global Meeting of the Hunger Project in New York City, is reprinted with permission of The Hunger Project.

Excerpt from *A Way of Being* by Carl Rogers, copyright 1980 by Houghton Mifflin Company, is reprinted with permission of Houghton Mifflin Company.

Excerpt from *Dialogue: Turning Controversy into Community* by Rachael A. Poliner and Jeffrey Benson, copyright 1997 by Educators for Social Responsibility, is reprinted with permission of Educators for Social Responsibility.

**Copyright © 2002 by Carl Zaiss**

All rights reserved. No part of this publication may be reproduced, distributed, or transmitted in any form or by any means, including photocopying, recording, or other electronic or mechanical methods, without the prior written permission of the publisher, except in the case of brief quotations embodied in critical reviews and certain other noncommercial uses permitted by copyright law or where permission is granted in the text. For permission requests, write to the publisher, addressed "Attention: Permissions Coordinator," at the address below.

Berrett-Koehler Publishers, Inc.

235 Montgomery Street, Suite 650

San Francisco, CA 94104-2916

Tel: (415) 288-0260 Fax: (415) 362-2512 www.bkconnection.com

**Ordering Information**

*Quantity sales.* Special discounts are available on quantity purchases by corporations, associations, and others. For details, contact the "Special Sales Department" at the Berrett-Koehler address above.

*Individual sales.* Berrett-Koehler publications are available through most bookstores. They can also be ordered direct from Berrett-Koehler: Tel: (800) 929-2929; Fax: (802) 864-7626; www.bkconnection.com

*Orders for college textbook/course adoption use.* Please contact Berrett-Koehler: Tel: (800) 929-2929; Fax: (802) 864-7626.

*Orders by U.S. trade bookstores and wholesalers.* Please contact Publishers Group West, 1700 Fourth Street, Berkeley, CA 94710. Tel: (510) 528-1444; Fax: (510) 528-3444.

**Printed in the United States of America**

Printed on acid-free and recycled paper that is composed of 50% recovered fiber, including 10% post consumer waste.

**Library of Congress Cataloging-in-Publication Data**

Zaiss, Carl D.
    True Partnership : revolutionary thinking about relating to others / Carl Zaiss.
      p. cm.
    Includes bibliographical references (p. )
    ISBN 1-57675-166-X
      1. Communication in organizations. 2. Interpersonal relations. 3. Social interaction.
I. Title.
HD30.3 .Z34 2001
650.1'3—dc21
                                               2001043697

**First Edition**

08  07  06  05  04  03  02          10  9  8  7  6  5  4  3  2  1

Interior Design & Illustration: Gopa Design & Illustration
Copy Editor: Kay Mikel, WordWorks      Proofreader: Henrietta Bensussen
Production: Linda Jupiter, Jupiter Productions    Indexer: Paula C. Durbin-Westby

14262

*To my family* —

Mickey

John, Zac, and Zoe

Scott

Kelly, David, Jayna, and Olivia

Brett and Serene

Mother and Walt

Linda

Anna

— *may we all experience the magnificent power of true partnership in our lives.*

And to Dad and Craig,
for all the lives you touched while you were with us.

# TABLE OF CONTENTS

# Foreword

*By Alfonso Montuori, Ph.D.*

IN THE INTRODUCTION OF this book, Carl Zaiss writes:

The main reason people don't accomplish more is that we fail to focus on what really matters—the quality of our relationships, which is shaped by the assumptions and beliefs we bring to the table, how we speak and how we listen, and how we approach disagreements and conflicts.

He goes on to state that we are stuck in mediocrity but that in fact we can reach much higher. By transforming our relationships, we will open up a world of possibilities. In this book, Carl Zaiss opens up that world of possibilities for us.

The term *partnership* can mean many things. It refers to relationships with vendors, limited partnerships, business alliances, the emphasis on teamwork, and a new spirit of seeking out opportunities for collaboration and networking. But partnership the way it is presented here is much more than a fashionable new buzzword. It literally calls for a complete shift in the way we view and, above all, *create* human relationships.

Once a decision is made to work together, the way in which that decision is implemented and the style of the interactions are key to the success of the enterprise. The desire to partner is not enough. Many efforts collapse because the participants have a mind-set that actively sabotages partnership. In *From Power to Partnership* (HarperCollins, 1993) Isabella Conti and I stressed that having a relationship, or "partnering," is not enough. It's the *quality* of the relationship that counts, whether in relationships with vendors, subordinates, bosses, neighbors, family members, or spouses. It is important to differentiate between a *real partnership*, a mutually beneficial relationship in which both parties win, and what, following Riane Eisler, we call a *dominator relationship*, which is just a convenient opportunity to work together, and where the quality of the relationship still focuses on zero-sum, win–lose relations. Unless this distinction is clarified and ground rules are established around the quality of relationship, the term *partnership* will just mean "working together" dominator-style. But, as Carl Zaiss shows us, it can mean much more than that. It is a worldview that embraces mind-set, values, behaviors, and interactions.

Most people respond with excitement to this alternative way of relating. They are justly tired of the old, power-oriented way of relating, and they are relieved to imagine a different world, a different society, and different institutions inspired by the idea of partnership as a foundation for interaction.

But the process needs to be taken beyond a critique of the old and visioning of the new. We must not only start to sketch what this world of partnership would look like but begin to develop actionable steps toward creating it. When we question the underlying assumptions of people's ideas of partnership, what partnership would mean in their workplace, it becomes clear why it's so hard to get beyond the old system. Most people believe partnership means no competition, no conflicts, no disagreement, and no real leadership. In groups set up to explore the idea of partnership, I have often heard comments such as "I saw my group was having a problem [during the discussion], but I didn't say anything because I didn't want to be a dominator."

The assumption behind this comment is that partnership means some kind of homogeneous, wishy-washy, milquetoast world where nobody expresses differences or disagreements, nobody takes leadership roles, and everybody is always "nice." This is profoundly misleading. Partnership is then too easily dismissed as unrealistic and the dominator belief system is one more time reaffirmed as "unfortunately" the only workable option.

As Carl Zaiss shows, putting partnership into action is not necessarily easy. We're not talking about a quick fix here or some kind of magic solution to all our problems. (Then again, when was the last time one of those magic quick fixes really worked?) It requires a shift in our thinking that may initially seem counterintuitive. But it may be getting easier! In my consulting work over the last ten years, I have noticed a distinctive and welcome shift in behavior in the workplace. I have come across less and less "office politics," less overt jockeying for power, less Machiavellianism. Don't get me wrong, I'm not suggesting they have disappeared completely or that everybody has suddenly become virtuous and angelic. And, to be sure, until recently a healthy economy didn't hurt. But overall it has been striking to me that the focus on power has diminished, and I have seen many organizations actively reject selfish, power-oriented behavior. It clearly goes against the culture. What could this mean? Have we reached a level of collective cultural and psychological intelligence where we have moved away from a power orientation?

The Global Values Survey conducted by Robert Inglehart at the University of Michigan suggests that there is a global shift toward partnership values. Inglehart's survey of forty-three countries shows that a substantial segment of the global population has shifted from a concern with basic survival and, therefore, with the accumulation of wealth and power, to a concern for well-being and quality of life. As Inglehart puts it, the survey shows a shift from Modern to Postmodern values, which he summarizes as a shift from Materialism to Postmaterialism, and from survival values to well-being values.

Unfortunately there are still many places, and many millions of people, who by necessity have to focus mainly on survival. But where there has been a shift away from power-oriented politics and eco-

nomics to greater economic democracy, this shift of values has already
begun to have an effect in the world of work. This has far-reaching
implications and is a force of potentially profound transformation.

If survival is my primary and all-encompassing value, I will work
hard to ensure that I have enough money to buy the essentials, and
I will struggle to get into a position where I can make sure I get these
essentials no matter what. If, on the other hand, my economic security is not the single overriding factor dominating my life, I can
begin to think about what else I want in life above and beyond a job
that will feed my stomach. I will literally look for other things to feed
me, to feed my mind, my heart and soul, and my senses.

Today more and more people reject workplaces that do not
reflect their values, or provide them with meaningful work. People
simply don't want to work in an environment that is unpleasant,
where there is constant tension and fighting and bickering and
backbiting. We realize that such behavior is stressful, selfish, and
ultimately does not enhance anyone's well-being.

It is this mind shift that Zaiss outlines so skillfully in these pages.
In a style that is simple and easy to read, but never simplistic, Zaiss
carefully shows us the elements of a partnership perspective and
presents its key principles. In this short and thoughtful book, the
reader will find much to think about, but even more that is actionable. And, the greater the understanding of the key principles, the
greater the capacity to put partnership into action.

Carl Zaiss has written a very timely book, one that will resonate
with all those who want to leave the dreary age of power politics
behind and move toward the creativity of partnership.

Alfonso Montuori, Ph.D.

August 2001

ALFONSO MONTUORI is a consultant with Lisardco, a leading
San Francisco Bay Area executive development firm, and an
associate professor at the California Institute of Integral Studies.
He is the author of numerous books and articles on creativity,
management, and social change.

# Preface

FOR MORE THAN THIRTY YEARS I have questioned what makes some people, some families, and some organizations more successful than others. My background includes sixteen years in sales, operations, and general management in both field and home positions in corporate America. Also, for the past eighteen years I have provided training and consulting services to a variety of clients throughout the United States, Canada, and Europe. I have worked with people from different cultures and different types of companies and different industries and different departments, and in organizations both large and small, and, yet, I have seen similar patterns everywhere.

From this varied experience, it has become obvious to me that we waste an inordinate amount of human potential in our organizations. Communication breakdowns and relationship issues with customers, between departments, and between layers of management continue to limit an organization's ability to compete effectively. Morale suffers from increased frustration, resentment, complacency, and cynicism.

Likewise, personal relationships seem to be strained, and we sense that more is available in even our closest and most intimate relationships. Communication issues among family members increase stress, tension, and unhappiness and damage the bonds in these essential relationships.

Day in and day out I speak with people who have a sense that there is so much more possible. These are people just like you and me who are frustrated with the existing systems at home and at work. We go to bed at night thinking about how much more we could have accomplished if only other people had done what needed doing. We spend a tremendous amount of time talking to others about how to deal with problems and issues presented by our children, spouses, bosses, clients, and others. The quality of our relationships seems to be a deep and natural concern for all of us.

Many solutions to the core issue of personal and organizational effectiveness have been presented, discussed, and implemented. We grab onto almost anything in hopes of finding solutions that work. The billions of dollars spent on personal and organizational fix-its show our hunger for something more. Most of these approaches have some effect, but none are nearly as significant or sustainable as what is needed and what is possible. It is almost as if we don't know that we don't know what the real source of the problem is.

My experience has led me to believe we have been looking in the wrong place. For the most part we are unaware of what is possible for our families, our organizations, and ourselves. My goal is to contribute to the existing body of knowledge on the subject of individual and organizational effectiveness by focusing on what really matters in producing results—the quality of our relationships. The principles and practices described in this book were not developed in a classroom. They are not based on esoteric theory about the way the world should be. They are not a secret formula. These principles and practices were developed in the trenches, in the everyday interactions with family, friends, and work associates that influence the quality of our lives. These principles and practices represent my extensive inquiry into the question of how to build and maintain more effective relationships with the people we live and work with.

This book is not *the truth*. This is a report on my journey, my experience. It represents my point of view and is designed to challenge and stimulate your thinking. This book will give you the opportunity to examine the automatic and habitual ways of thinking and behaving that shape the quality and effectiveness of your relationships and provides another viewpoint—a new way of seeing—that has enhanced the relationships of many people. I encourage you to *try it on* and then decide for yourself.

In Chapter One we will examine the assumptions and beliefs of the traditional manner in which we relate to one another. In Chapter Two we will build a new framework based on four principles of true partnership: connecting, communicating, expanding, and observing. Each of these four principles will then be addressed individually in Chapters Three through Six. Finally, in Chapter Seven we will look at what you and I can do as individuals to bring true partnership from possibility to reality in our day-to-day living.

I love watching people find greater levels of love, joy, happiness, and accomplishment. If I can demonstrate ways to make something else available that enhances your relationships with others and therefore your success in life, I will have accomplished my objective.

*True Partnership* does not merely offer improvements in our relationships, it signals a significant shift in the way we communicate with and relate to people around us.

## ACKNOWLEDGMENTS

This book represents my own tremendous personal growth and development and it could not have happened without incredible support from others. The idea for this book was originally conceived in March 1995 during a lunch with my friend Alison Armstrong. She had been my coach and trusted confidant while writing my first book, *Sales Effectiveness Training,* and we were discussing how that book had opened a big door into the concept of partnership. Out of that conversation came my commitment to continue my exploration of partnership.

Others have contributed to that process as well. Veda Stram provided perhaps the greatest contribution as an editor, proofreader, and "wordsmith." She spent countless hours reading and re-reading the manuscript. She kept me on track and focused on what needed to be said and added a great deal to the framework of the book. In addition, Richard Basch, Ann Bauer, Rex Coble, Brook Cross, Rick Davis, Lew and Francine Epstein, Linda Garner, David and Nancy Grundman, Julia McCarthy, Rose Owens, Chris Parker, Todd Reid, Mark Siegfried, Rolland and Sharon Todd, and David Welsch all contributed seemingly endless hours of discussion and dialogue. In each conversation new insights emerged as we confronted and challenged my initial beliefs, causing me to expand my frame of reference.

I also want to acknowledge my clients who, by applying the principles and practices of true partnership and creating miracles in their lives, fueled my passion and commitment to the project.

Two men have made significant contributions to my work. One is Dr. Thomas Gordon, author of several books, including *Parent Effectiveness Training* and *Leader Effectiveness Training*. We worked together for several years designing and delivering Synergistic Selling, an innovative sales training program that has made a significant impact on many salespeople and sales organizations. From Tom, I learned the importance of focusing on the relationship in improving individual and organizational performance.

The other man is someone I have never met personally, but he has had a significant impact on my work. Werner Erhard is the founder of what is now Landmark Education Corporation, and I participated in the Forum and other programs offered through Landmark for many years. From Werner's work I learned the power of the context that we bring to the table in each and every interaction we have with others.

I acknowledge both of these men, and those who teach their principles, for their contribution to humanity. Because of my in-depth experience with the work of Tom Gordon and Werner Erhard, I am who I am today. Some readers may also be familiar with their programs and may notice their influence on my work.

Please keep in mind that any similarity comes from my interpretation of what they provide.

Then, of course, there is Steve Piersanti and the team at Berrett-Koehler. I first talked to Steve about this project five years ago. Even at that early stage of development he was able to see small nuggets of value. More recently, he has provided tremendous editorial support and challenged me to examine in even greater detail the fine points of true partnership. I appreciate his trust and confidence in my ability to take his feedback and put it into practice. In addition, Berrett-Koehler forwarded the completed manuscript to five reviewers: Kathleen Epperson, Jean Ortiz, Joseph Wolf, Perviz Randeria, and Jennifer Myers. I want to thank them for the manner in which they reviewed the manuscript and the contributions they made to the final product.

Finally, a special thanks and acknowledgment to my fiancée and partner for life, Mickey Glassman. Not only have our conversations significantly influenced the final manuscript, but she also provided the day-by-day support that enabled me to make my vision a reality.

Carl Zaiss
*Clifton, Virginia*
*February 2002*

# Revolutionary Thinking about the Nature of Our Relationships

*To experiment with one's life is not going to
be everyone's choice. It is too risky. That is sad,
because we are then condemned to live in boxes
we made for ourselves or let others make for us.*
—Charles Handy

WE ARE ALL CAPABLE OF PRODUCING far more than we do either by ourselves or with others. The very nature of our relationships limits our ability to accomplish all that is really possible. Some relationships do provide love and support in our lives, but for the most part our traditional manner of relating to others works against us. When we realize that what is absolutely necessary is a critical reassessment of our basic thinking about relationships and the profound impact they have on our success, something amazing happens.

At a meeting with Karen, a training manager with a major hotel company, I presented the core concepts of my work. She replied, "I disagree. I don't worry about my relationships. What kept me up last night was the meeting I have with my boss tomorrow about how to work closer with the field sales organization so they are happier with the training we provide."

I was thunderstruck. She didn't even hear herself talking about relationships—with her boss and with the field sales organization. She was focusing on what was wrong and how to fix it rather than on the quality of those relationships. We are so conditioned to solve problems, increase sales, and improve profitability that we fail to address what really matters in producing results—the quality of our relationships. When confronted with improving individual and organizational effectiveness, we do not even know where to look, and we don't know that we don't know.

Results are the outcomes of actions. When we want to improve results, we typically look at how to change actions. We develop a new strategy. In reality, these actions—our behavior—and the results we produce are shaped by the quality of our relationships. Extraordinary improvements in performance and results are possible when we focus on and fundamentally alter the nature of our relationships.

One of the most common strategies for improving our ability to live and work together is to build a partnership. In the business environment, the term *partnership* is used as a marketing or management strategy as in "becoming partners with your customers." And everywhere in our society, we hear of groups of people working together in a "partnership for this" and a "partnership for that." At home we are told that marriage should be a partnership. Yet most partnerships do not access what is truly possible. Due to the basic nature of our relationships, our partnerships are often superficial and ineffective.

Several years ago I was facilitating a program on partnership for one of my clients. To kick off the workshop, my client had asked their top customer to address the sales team to set the stage for the day's activities about partnership. You can imagine their surprise when the customer said to this group: "To us, your customer, partnership is just another ploy to get into our pockets. It's nothing more than a new sales gimmick." Obviously something was missing between the intention of my client and the experience of the customer.

Sadly, even the concept of partnership has been reduced to one of many techniques or strategies to improve organizational performance. As such, it has become shallow and simplistic, with limited impact. As a result, today most partnerships are pretty much cosmetic in nature.

Many people think they already understand partnership. The generally accepted perception is that it is a form of relationship where people work together to accomplish a common goal. Partnership is thought to be a fifty-fifty proposition with both sides willing to collaborate and contribute equally. Others see partnership in a legal or financial sense, and still others see it as a strategic relationship, an alliance.

Most of what we call partnership is not. "True partnership" is a higher order of relatedness generated by a shift in the way we, as individuals, see the world. True partnership is a *state of mind*, not a type of relationship. It is a *framework of relating to others* that has an impact on every interaction.

Many people assume that it takes two people to make partnership happen. What if this is not the case? What if true partnership is an individual phenomenon? What if a successful relationship is one in which individuals operate *from* true partnership rather than *in* partnership?

True partnership is not nirvana, utopia, or heaven on earth. It is a new way of looking at the world that provides access to solutions for issues and problems not apparent to most people, and at the same time it also opens the door to new opportunities that we do not know exist. As an example, by shifting the view of the world from "the earth is flat" to "the earth is round," people were able to access a myriad of new solutions to existing problems and literally discover a *whole new world*.

The purpose of this book is to articulate a new context, a whole new world. True partnership represents a fundamental transformation, a paradigm shift in our approach to relating to others. It is a *paradigm-altering* approach. It is not about tips and techniques, the trendy how-to's that most people look for. Tips and techniques are ways to get better within a familiar paradigm; they are *paradigm-enhancing* tools. True partnership requires altering the way we perceive the world. "In the long run, nothing short of a complete transformation of the way people perceive and process reality will do" (Eisler 1987, 2).

When people learn to master the principles and practices of true partnership, they discover that they have new tools for resolving issues and forming highly effective relationships. Unlike the superficial approach to partnership, true partnership provides an unprecedented opportunity to alter the fundamental thinking that shapes the quality of our relationships, the effectiveness of our interactions, and the results we produce. With a solid understanding of and appreciation for true partnership, we are better prepared to cope with the challenges and issues we face. "There are solutions to the major problems of our time, some of them even simple. But they require a radical shift in our perception, our thinking, our values" (Capra 1996, 4).

This is not a distinction to be taken lightly.

## THE CHALLENGES WE FACE

By creating a true partnership perspective and transforming the way we relate to others, we can discover new solutions to some of the challenges and issues we face:

- People desire greater satisfaction, enjoyment, and accomplishment from their relationships at home and at work.
- Families require a new quality of relatedness due to changing family structures.
- Organizations find it increasingly more difficult to accomplish their purpose and search for a new sense of collaboration and teamwork.
- Communities face critical social issues that call for a fundamental shift in our capacity to deal with complex issues.

- Nations must find new ways of relating to each other that fulfills our need for sustainable peace, cooperation, and security in our world.

We are spending a great deal of time, effort, and money in attempts to resolve these seemingly different issues, but they are all related. They are symptoms of a common problem—the nature of our relationships. Let's examine each of these challenges in more detail.

*People desire greater satisfaction, enjoyment, and accomplishment from their relationships at home and at work.*

There is a growing desire by many of us to attain a new level of personal satisfaction and productivity that we have not been able to achieve no matter how much we improve our personal effectiveness. Our hearts are in the right place: We want better relationships, we want to accomplish more, we want to grow. But we bump into seemingly immovable obstacles—usually other people—and become resigned to the status quo. We are left with a sense of isolation, a feeling of helplessness, a loss of connection.

In our personal lives we want greater joy, happiness, and satisfaction. We want to move beyond the pain of broken marriages and unresolved conflicts. We want stronger bonds between parents and children of all ages. And we want greater support from those around us for our own goals and aspirations. Most of all, we want stronger connections with those we love to help compensate for the complex and fast-paced world in which we live.

In the workplace, most of us are capable of producing far more than we do. We leave work feeling we could have accomplished more. We talk openly about our hands being tied and about being limited in our ability to move through the obstacles inherent in the organization. Every day we see committed and talented people frustrated and thwarted in their attempts to achieve organizational and personal goals.

We want a more peaceful and productive work environment. We strive for reduced conflict, less tension, and increased cooperation and productivity. Many people talk about their frustrations with "the system." They want to improve performance but can't get the accounting department—or the sales department, the marketing department, manufacturing, senior management, or the board of directors—to do what they think needs to be done. Oftentimes, widespread resignation, complacency, and cynicism often dominate the workplace. This results in a tremendous waste of the human potential available in our organizations. It dampens the spirit and saps the energy and passion of our most valuable asset—people.

*Families require a new quality of relatedness due to changing family structures.*

The breakdown of the basic family unit has led to greater demands on our communication and relationships between family members. The stereotypical picture of the family that existed just a generation or so ago is nearly extinct. Rarely do we see Mom and Dad staying married and raising their children, with Dad working and Mom staying home with the kids. What we do see are broken families being merged together into new units, dual income families with both parents working, single parents raising children on their own, and more mobile families being separated from the security of the extended family.

Furthermore, time with our families must be carved out of increasingly complex schedules with even more distractions, leaving many children feeling isolated and lost. At the same time, the family faces challenging circumstances such as the prevalence of drugs, the barrage of sex and violence in the media, and the lack of quality education. All of these result in increased pressure and instability on family relationships, and most of us lack the skills to live effectively in this new environment.

*Organizations find it increasingly more difficult to accomplish their purpose and search for a new sense of collaboration and teamwork.*

The hypercompetitive global marketplace demands a highly productive and effective workforce. Organizations of all types from international conglomerates to entrepreneurial startups, nonprofit organizations, academic institutions, trade and professional associations, and local and national governments are looking for new ways to improve the results their people produce. Many leaders seem to know there is tremendous underutilized potential, and they are frustrated, if not stymied, with the unworkability of customary solutions.

People complain about the absence of leadership, the declining work ethic, the frantic pace of business, the demands for entitlements, and the limited education of many workers. These are issues that ordinary approaches to empowerment do not seem to touch, leaving management teams wondering what is really needed.

Leaders in organizations must find new ways to create work environments that foster the development of people and fulfill the often spoken but seldom delivered commitment that "people are our greatest asset." It takes more than fancy, well-worded mission statements and motivational slogans to meet the challenges of today's global marketplace.

*Communities face critical social issues that call for a fundamental shift in our capacity to deal with complex issues.*

Crime, homelessness, and drug abuse continue to permeate our communities. Environmental concerns, an overburdened judicial system, gun control, health care, campaign financing, and other pertinent issues are not being resolved. People working to solve community and social problems want a breakthrough in dealing with other human beings. As individuals we yearn for new skills to deal with and resolve complex issues so we can accomplish more and feel better about our efforts. The challenge of finding workable solutions is not getting any easier.

We are not prepared for the whole new class of problems and global issues that we undoubtedly will face in the next few decades. It is likely that by the year 2015 an additional one billion people will inhabit our planet. It is expected that ninety-five percent of this population growth will occur in developing nations. This will cause problems of resource allocation that most of us today cannot even begin to comprehend.

During a recent panel discussion on CNN regarding hunger and homelessness, individuals on the panel represented three different nonprofit groups. They debated the *right* way to address these problems, and it seemed obvious to me that many good resources were going to waste because these organizations were not collaborating. The squabbling over who was right and who was wrong was intolerable to watch and did nothing to move them closer to solving these critical issues.

*Nations must find new ways of relating to each other that fulfills our need for sustainable peace, cooperation, and security in our world.*

We are a global community. Yet, there appears to be very little cooperation in resolving the issues our community faces. In some cases we do partner together to defeat a common foe but there is very little ongoing effort to resolve the political and religious differences that create regional conflicts and wars to begin with. We still utilize a Stone Age mentality in resolving conflicts—only our weapons are more sophisticated and treacherous. The costs in human terms are simply too great to continue down the same path.

The difference between the haves and the have-nots continues to grow. While hundreds of millions of people enjoy a lifestyle of affluence, health, and security, the vast majority of the world's population lives with unfathomable poverty, disease, and fear. Then, we wonder why resentment, crime, fanaticism, and terrorism permeate our world. When people don't have the basic needs for survival met, they must look somewhere to release their anger.

Today, the very sustainability of our planet's future is in quesiton.

## SOMETHING IS MISSING

Today we have technology that makes instantaneous communication possible nearly anywhere on the planet. In fact, individuals and organizations are drowning in a flood of email, voice mail, faxes, and wireless phone calls. Yet, in our world of high-tech communication, there seems to be little real connection. We might communicate more quickly and with greater frequency, but we do so without contributing to the fundamental worth of the relationship or resolving some of the issues we face.

It just seems that much more is possible. Deep inside, many people share this same feeling. Listen to almost any conversation about families, organizations, or government and you will hear people expressing dissatisfaction with the status quo and their deep sense that things could be better. We waste a great deal of time, effort, and money on strategies for improving performance that fail to produce the intended outcomes. The result? We are all left with a deep sense that something is missing and that something else is possible.

The main reason that people don't accomplish more, or that we don't move beyond the challenges we face, is that we fail to focus on what really matters—the quality of our relationships. Our relationships are shaped by the assumptions and beliefs we bring to the table, how we speak and how we listen, and how we approach disagreements and conflicts.

True partnership is a new context, a new way of seeing the world. It provides a new perspective to view the challenges, a new approach to problem solving, new solutions, new opportunities, and a new quality to our relationships. True partnership also provides a solid foundation for existing strategies for improving performance to have the impact they were designed to have. The principles and practices of true partnership are a pathway to a whole new dimension of individual and organizational effectiveness.

The revolutionary change to a true partnership perspective will not happen by mandate, election, or prescription. We cannot wait for others. The job of transforming our families, our organizations, our society, and ourselves is up to each of us. True partnership will live only when we each embrace it and put it into action. The conversion to a true partnership perspective is an individual choice. It happens one individual at a time. "Throughout history, the really fundamental changes in societies have come about not from dictates of governments and the results of battles, but through vast numbers of people changing their minds—sometimes just a little bit" (Harman 1998, viii).

Is this choice for you?

# 1 THE DRIFT AND HOW IT SHAPES OUR ACTIONS

*It is hard to find any institution in modern society—business, government, public education, the family—that is not suffering breakdown.* —Peter Senge

The context shapes our thinking and our actions. The traditional context in which we relate to each other—what I call the drift—is grounded in power and control. This drift, based on who has the power in the relationship and who does not, shapes our interactions with one another. Most people are unaware of it and respond instinctively with predictable patterns of behavior. Once we recognize these patterns, we are more able to move beyond them. Solutions designed to enhance individual and organizational performance that do not alter the drift rarely produce the intended results.

TO UNDERSTAND HOW THE DRIFT SHAPES OUR ACTIONS, we must first recognize the difference between context and content. The *American Heritage Dictionary* defines *context* as "the circumstances in which a particular event occurs," and *content* as "that which is contained in a receptacle." In other words, context is the frame of reference—the space in which content shows up. Once we master this distinction, we will discover new opportunities for more effective action. When we realize the power of changing a context, we will become more proactive and less a victim of circumstances. By distinguishing the difference between context and content, we open the door to whole new dimensions and discover that we have more influence on the quality of our lives than we thought.

Without a basic understanding and appreciation of context, our attempts to change our present condition remain focused on more "stuff," more content within the existing paradigm. For example, if I say these words—bomber, submarine, torpedo, and hero—what do you think of first? Most people think of the military or of war. However, if I add the word "hoagie," the context changes. Now what are you thinking about? Most people think about sandwiches. You could not develop a better submarine sandwich inside a military context. Sometimes one piece of new information can fundamentally alter the context, giving the content a different meaning and therefore providing for different actions.

Context is a frame of reference. It can be an individual's mindset or the organizational culture. Context is our perception of the facts or data of content. It shapes the way we view people, situations, and events in our lives. It is the invisible environment in the background of every interaction and it shapes the outcomes.

In a 1988 speech titled "Altering an Era," Joan Holmes, executive director of the Hunger Project, said that "[i]t is the era, the climate of our times that limits and shapes our way of being. The climate of our times, our era, determines what we see as being possible, and it determines what we see as being achievable." Later she added, "We need to remember that the person we are talking to is the product of a climate. That person is only thinking that which is allowed in this climate. So it's easier to be frustrated with that person than with the climate. When a new climate allows that person to think something different, he or she will, because we are all a product of a climate that allows certain thoughts."

When Holmes refers to "the era, the climate of our times," she is talking about context. The context that we operate from is based on our particular perspective and underlying beliefs and assumptions. It is the context that shapes our behavior, the results we produce, and what we judge to be possible or not possible.

A context can be created out of a group of shared understandings, and our individual perspective is shaped by these larger contexts. Our families and organizations each have unique cultures. Furthermore, our ethnic heritage, religious background, gender, age, geographic history, economic status, and social community all instill shared beliefs that shape the personal context for our lives. For example, Americans living in the present time have a totally different context for their lives than those who lived in the eighteenth century. A woman living in Kansas City has a different context from a woman living in Singapore. And a woman living in Los Angeles has a different perspective from a man living in Los Angeles.

These group contexts become the cultural norms that influence our perception and our behavior. This is especially true when we consider the basic need of most humans to fit in or to conform. Most of us will tend to think and act as others would with a similar cultural background in similar circumstances, thus, the power of context. A context then becomes the invisible background that shapes every aspect of our lives.

Context is generally inherited. I like to refer to this as *the drift* as it describes the assumptions and beliefs that we take for granted and that shape our world as we float through life. It takes us in a direction of its choosing rather than our own. The drift is different for each of us, but the fundamental nature of the drift is the same. It defines who we are and how we see the world. It limits our possibilities by conditioning us to think and act in certain ways, leaving us unaware of different perspectives, different options. The drift determines what is appropriate and what is not—and what is possible and what is not. Unless we as individuals consciously intervene in the natural flow of the drift, it determines the flow of our lives. This process isn't inherently wrong, but it is certainly limiting.

From my years of experience working with people in many different organizations and different cultures, I realized that human beings generally have certain things in common. There seems to be a framework of thinking common to all of us, that transcends race, religion, gender, and all other factors in our personal histories. In other words, although each of us is a unique individual due to our different past experiences, we all share some common ways of thinking that transcend race, gender, and other cultural differences.

Knowing that paradigms influence the context we live in, I began looking for the paradigms that might shape contemporary thinking. I was surprised to discover the magnitude of the impact that the science of physics has had on our thinking and behavior. Our thinking patterns and, beyond that, our patterns of relationship are shaped by many of the same laws and principles that form the foundation of the science of physics. Physics is the study of the natural or physical world, and it seems that human beings are as affected by the laws of physics as are subatomic particles. You don't have to be a scientist or an expert in physics to understand the fundamentals: "The whole world of matter, including our own bodies, is made up of atoms and their even smaller components, and the laws that govern these tiny bits of basic reality spill over into our daily lives" (Zohar 1990, 21).

In his groundbreaking work *The Turning Point*, Fritjof Capra (1982, 53) writes, "Between 1500 and 1700 there was a dramatic shift in the way people pictured their world and their whole way of thinking." This shift came as a result of the development of a new model of physical reality constructed by Sir Isaac Newton (1642–1727), and it has been an invisible influence in shaping all aspects of our lives for over three hundred years.

Through his insights, Newton developed a new model of the world and a set of rules and laws that would explain his model. Newtonian physics is based on a mechanical model of the universe that reduces all reality to basic parts: atoms and particles. Each part is fundamentally separate from other parts and connected only by external forces of energy. The Newtonian paradigm is based on individualism, separateness, cause and effect, either–or thinking, and a fixed view of reality. Newtonian objects that meet must collide and go their separate ways. It is a model that focuses on individual entities and the forces of attraction and repulsion between those entities.

Using this paradigm as the context for our relationships—as most of us do, whether we realize it or not—we view other people as objects, or things. We see ourselves as separate entities, different from one another. As a result, we assume we must either be in control or be controlled by other people. Often we automatically approach situations combatively to protect our interests or to avoid feeling dominated. Relationships become about colliding or avoiding collisions with others.

## CHARACTERISTICS OF THE DRIFT

These principles of the Newtonian paradigm influence the way we observe the world and form the current context, or framework, of our relationships with others. This context shapes what we say and what we don't say, how we listen or don't listen to others, our actions and all of the results we produce. This paradigm has four fundamental characteristics:

- We see ourselves as separate, autonomous individuals.
- We see ourselves as connected to others through forces of power and control.
- We operate from an either–or mentality.
- We relate to the world as a fixed and predetermined place.

It is important to examine the assumed and unquestioned structures that form this paradigm. As long as the structures are taken for granted and remain invisible and unexamined, we are stuck and powerless. Only when we question the invisible assumptions that form the context that has such a tremendous influence over our behavior will we have the capacity to change. Let's look at how each of these characteristics shows up in our daily lives.

## Separate, Autonomous Individuals

Since we see ourselves in this Newtonian model as independent islands in a sea of humanity, we must prove that we can make it on our own and protect our independence. Independence is what we have aimed at and have been acknowledged for all of our lives. From learning to walk, to tying our shoes, to reciting the ABCs, to riding a bike or driving a car, most of the highlights in our lives occur when we have learned to do things on our own. We relish and love our independence; Americans especially grow up valuing the stoic independent John Wayne way of life—the *"I can do it on my own"* individualistic mentality.

When we focus on the individual, we embrace certain assumptions. How many of these ideas do you recognize?

- We live in the illusion that we have only ourselves to rely on, and our need for control is amplified.
- We emphasize the importance of self-development, building on our strengths and overcoming our weaknesses.
- We think of other people in terms of their identity, their personality, and, at work, as their title or position.
- We view relationships from a personality perspective: "Do I or do I not like you?" "Are you my type of person?"
- We develop a mask to look good and be more acceptable to others, and then we avoid taking off the mask and being vulnerable.
- We protect our identity and individuality by building walls between ourselves and other people.
- We do not allow others to get past our walls and they don't let us past theirs.
- We blame the individual when things don't go as we want them to and try to fix others or ourselves.

When we relate to others and ourselves as autonomous individuals, we separate ourselves from them in these ways:

- We focus on the differences in people. Everything then becomes a comparison, and we rank people as superior or inferior based on the differences.
- We act as fragmented parts of the whole, without the big picture: "I'll do my job and you do yours."
- We isolate ourselves and eliminate any sense of intimacy in family, team, or organizational relationships.
- We set up a we–they orientation, an inherently adversarial relationship: men versus women, parents versus children, teachers versus students, Republican versus Democrat, management versus employees or the union, old timers versus new people, home office versus the field, sales versus operations, the company versus the customers.
- We blame others, and eliminate any sense of personal accountability.

### Connected to Others through Power and Control

Power and control—who has it and who doesn't—is in the background of almost all of our interactions whether we want to accept it or not. It could be called the default mechanism we fall back on; it shapes communication and outcomes. We often look at the world through a lens of power and control: Who has the power here? If it's not me, how can I get more power? It is not that we are into abusing power because we want to, but for the most part we don't know another way. Take the time to look at what's going on in many of your relationships. How often is it about dominating or avoiding the domination of others?

Look behind any conversation and you will find some version of *"There must be something I can do to get you to do what I want you to do."* It's just that some of us are more blatant, others more subtle, and others more charming. No matter how sophisticated the technique, however, when others are trying to change us, we resort to our own patterns for avoiding their attempts.

Here are some things that happen when we relate to others from a context of power and control:

- We set up many conversations as attempts to mold others' behavior and spend a great deal of time strategizing on what we can do to get them to change.
- We receive the communication of others thinking "it's just manipulation." Even organizational empowerment programs are seen by many as "just another form of them trying to get me to do what they want me to do."
- We try to get "buy-in" for our ideas, which sets up more attempts at manipulation.
- We avoid confrontations because conflicts are only seen as having a winner and a loser.
- We convert we–they thinking into power struggles that can only be resolved through someone winning and someone losing. Alternatively, they don't get resolved, and a stalemate occurs out of which nothing happens.
- We see compromise as the goal, where each gives up something to accommodate the other, with neither person being satisfied or committed to the outcome.
- We find ourselves in a game of reacting to the domination of other people, and our choices seem limited to three options: fight, flight, or submit.

When we fight, we
- find ways to use more power.
- look for ways to retaliate.
- go behind their backs, over their heads to their boss, or around them.
- form groups and alliances to balance the power.
- complain to others, gossip and/or ridicule others.
- openly resist the other person.

- threaten to quit a job or leave the relationship.
- take legal action.

When we choose flight, we
- leave the relationship, ask for a transfer, or leave the organization.
- stay in the relationship physically, but leave mentally.
- avoid the other person whenever and however possible.
- withdraw and don't contribute to the relationship, the family, the team, or the organization.

And, when we submit, we
- keep score.
- acquiesce our needs just to maintain harmony.
- get resigned, complacent, and/or cynical.
- harbor resentment and experience greater stress and burnout.
- do only what is necessary to get by as there is no reason or motivation to go the extra mile.
- feel powerless and inadequate, which affects our self-esteem and self-worth.

One fundamental premise of the power and control context is that in the arena of interpersonal relationships, losers resent winners. If you win in an interaction with another person at their expense—they lose—they will resent you. This resentment then manifests itself in through the fight, flight, and submit options. It is this resentment inside of our relationships that undermines personal effectiveness, family harmony, organizational productivity, community problem-solving, and international peace, cooperation, and stability.

The game of power and control is everywhere, and it is in the background of nearly all our relationships. Some people are very adept at playing this game, but the outcomes are costly to both the individual who exercises the power and the individual who does not. If you are coming from power and control, the other person will sense it and act accordingly. No amount of people skills will make a difference.

## An Either–Or Mentality

It always seems to be one way or the other. You may have already noticed this thinking by your reaction to the first two segments of this chapter. For example, many of us do not like to consider any option that does not protect our individuality, as we think that someone is asking us to forgo our individuality. In other words it feels like we either have our independence or we don't. Likewise, when someone asks us to give up our power and control orientation, we hear it as being asked to be powerless and not in control.

For the most part this principle manifests itself in our right–wrong view of the world—"There is a right way to do this and a wrong way!"—and mostly it is *our* way that is the right way. When we are being right, we speak as if our opinion—our point of view—is the truth. We forget that it is simply our opinion. Our efforts at being right are apparent everywhere. We win arguments through the use of our power or our position, with overwhelming evidence, by creating an alliance with other people who agree with us, and by never admitting to being wrong.

The outcome of acting as if we are right, however, is that we make the other person wrong. When you and I feel we are being made wrong, we get defensive about our position and either withdraw and shut down or go on the offensive and counterattack. One thing is certain, when we feel we are made wrong, we hesitate in sharing our thoughts and opinions and cease to fully participate in the relationship.

This right–wrong orientation in interpersonal communication is very limiting and often results in nothing being accomplished.

- We compare other people to what we think is right and alienate ourselves from those we perceive as being wrong.

- We make the typical conversation a debate over who is right and who is not. Conversations become debates wherein someone wins and someone loses. There is very little listening going on. Instead, people are simply trying to pick apart each other's opinions so they can come out on top.
- We waste a great deal of time and effort just to prove that we are right.
- We blame others for the lack of results so we don't have to be wrong.
- We become positional and get stuck protecting our opinions and then nothing gets resolved.

Here are some other ways that either–or thinking limits our effectiveness:

- *Authoritative or permissive.* To avoid being seen as authoritative and dictatorial, many of us go to the other extreme and become passive. We neither take a stand nor powerfully communicate our needs, wants, desires, or point of view.
- *Agree or disagree.* We tend to listen to others from an agree–disagree standpoint, noticing only whether or not there is agreement with what was said. No attempt is made to simply understand the other's opinion.
- *Individualism or collectivism.* We think that it has to be one or the other. As a result, many of us think we will lose our individuality by being part of a group. This is one of the factors that limits group effectiveness.
- *Results or satisfying relationships.* Most conversations center on one or the other, and the assumption (not always stated) is that you can't have both. It seems that you have to be nice to build the relationship but *not nice* to get results.
- *Short-term or long-term results.* Listen to any conversation about results and you will hear that you must give up one to attain the other. Nearly all new strategies revolve around this

point of view. Mostly it shows up in conversations when someone mentions the demands of Wall Street. There seems to be little opportunity to create something that can have an impact both on short-term profitability and on long-term growth of the company.

## A Fixed and Predetermined World

We see the world and especially other people as fixed entities that are precisely defined—"*That's just the way he/she/it is.*" That's just the way Bob is. That's just the way Mary is. That's just the way my mother-in-law is. That's just the way teenagers are. That's just the way the market is. That's just the way accounting is. That's just the way salespeople are. That's just the way men are. That's just the way women are. We see people as having fixed identities and predictable patterns of behavior, and many of our relationships are played out within these specified boundaries. We value certainty and strive for it and tend to notice only those actions that prove that people and groups of people are the way we see them. We are not open to alternatives.

Many of us live in a box we could label "I'm doing the best I can considering the circumstances," and we view the circumstances to be as solid as cement. As a result, many of us live in resignation, complacency, or even anger because we feel powerless in the face of the circumstances of our lives.

When we relate to the world as fixed and predetermined, we find ourselves doing these things.

- We see ourselves as fixed identities with a personality over which we have little control. We act as if we were born lazy, ambitious, committed, funny, serious, introverted, extroverted, flaky, or charming and assume that's the way we are and will always be.

- We freeze people into certain boxes and limit their ability to act differently. We say things like "my husband is controlling," "my daughter is lazy," "my mother-in-law is nosey," "my boss is demanding," or "my customer is stupid" as if it's the truth and they could never be different.
- We think we already know it all and limit our ability to be contributed to or coached by others and to learn and grow.
- We interact with people in the same manner we always have, which perpetuates the way they relate to us and thus validates our "that's just the way they are" thinking.
- We anticipate trouble with certain people or groups of people.
- We waste a lot of time in conversations about how to deal with others by always coming from the view that our judgments about them are correct.
- We rarely listen to or attempt to understand anyone who does not share our point of view.
- We have difficulty stepping beyond the status quo because we like it when people and events are predictable and conform to our expectations.

Having a fixed perception limits our ability to move beyond our present circumstances. Certain factors seem to be cast in cement as if nothing can be done about them.

## How the Drift Shapes Our Actions

We have identified the four basic characteristics of the drift:

- We see ourselves as separate, autonomous individuals: "I can do it on my own."
- We see ourselves as connected to others through forces of power and control: "There must be something I can do to get you to do what I want you to do."

- We operate from an either–or mentality: "There is a right way to do this and a wrong way."
- We relate to our world as fixed and predetermined: "That's just the way he/she/it is!"

Now let's take a look at how the drift shapes our thinking, our actions, and, therefore, the results we generate.

The drift becomes the framework of the box in which we live, and it is the basis for our belief that we can't do anything to change things because "that's just human nature." Picture a pair of glasses with the characteristics of the drift forming the lens. We then live our lives, raise our families, operate our businesses, and build our communities wearing those glasses. The drift shapes how we view others, how we react to others, what we say and don't say, how we listen, what we see as problems, what we consider to be viable solutions to those problems, and what we think is or is not achievable. We simply cannot see beyond what the drift allows us to see. And, if we can't see it, we cannot act on it.

Look inside most organizations and you will find talented and hard-working people thinking and acting in ways shaped by the drift. We are trained to follow the rules of the game, the prescribed and accepted behavior necessary for success. We battle over items particular to our function to protect our turf or advance our agenda. We actively strive to strengthen our power base, or we become experts at sniffing out the real power and go running to it. We make decisions based on who will like it or how easy it is to sell it, not on what would work. We deal more with the perceived political reality rather than the operational reality. And those of us who do not want to play this game get resigned, complacent, or even cynical, and many leave whether by our own choice or not.

Pretty much the same situation exists at home with the same consequences. Either we stay in the relationship with our resignation, complacency, or cynicism, or we leave the relationship completely.

The drift is the default mechanism that is in play whether we are aware of it or not. It is as if we are fish in an aquarium of dirty water. We take it for granted and don't know any better. We can't even see that the water is dirty—it's just the way life is. Only when we move to an aquarium where the water is clear do we realize how dirty the water was.

Most of us can relate to this in some form. We have all been in a relationship or a job that didn't work for us and we simply adapted to it. Pretty soon the pain went away because we thought it was normal. When we finally got out of the situation, for whatever reason, we looked back and were shocked that we had put up with what we did for as long as we did. Psychologists tell us that human beings often are willing to adapt to the pain of a known situation rather than take a risk and venture into the unknown.

Once you understand the power and limitations of the drift, you will clearly realize how actions within the drift have limited both personal satisfaction and organizational effectiveness. Using power and control or right–wrong thinking minimizes your ability to have a positive impact on the behavior of your customer, your employees, your spouse, or your children. This is exactly why most solutions and new initiatives to improve individual and team performance fail to produce the intended results. They fail to intervene with what's in the background shaping the results—the drift.

## THE LIMITATIONS OF TRADITIONAL SOLUTIONS

There is a tendency to grab hold of the latest self-help fad in hopes of finding a solution that works, and the billions of dollars spent on these "fix-its" show our hunger for something different. Yet something is missing. All our attempts to improve individual and organizational effectiveness come from a paradigm that is fundamentally flawed. They come from an ineffective place to start—the drift. These attempts are based on a certain set of assumptions and beliefs, the framework of the drift, and they form a very weak foundation on which to build any performance improvement initiative. As Albert Einstein is often quoted as saying, "The world we have made as a result of the level of thinking we have done so far creates problems we cannot solve at the same level of thinking at which we created them."

We have exhausted the personal-effectiveness paradigm in our personal lives. Self-help books are available on every conceivable subject. These books have spawned an entire billion-dollar industry with motivational audiotapes, videotapes, enthusiastic speakers, personal development seminars, and outdoor adventure programs. Some people have changed their lives and accomplished great things as a result of these programs. But at best these results are hit or miss or produce only incremental improvements.

Workplace solutions appear to be more sophisticated, but the results are the same. We restructure, reengineer, or reinvent the organization. We change who reports to whom. We decentralize decision making. We centralize decision making. We change the sales channel by realigning sales territories and/or the products they represent. We modify the paper flow. We change the names of the departments or people's titles. We endlessly reinvent organizational processes to be more effective.

We get training in how to do our job, manage our time, use automation, manage diversity, manage our boss, or handle upset customers. We learn interview techniques, sexual harassment legalities, team-building skills, goal setting, and on and on and on. Every year organizations spend billions of dollars on training designed to enhance performance. Today we have experts on everything. The marketplace is full of consulting firms and individual consultants, each with a unique approach to organizational change and performance improvement. Human resources executives get dozens of phone calls a week from individuals and companies offering a new approach. If we have so much wisdom available, why aren't we more satisfied and more effective?

Most attempts to change our families, our organizations, our society, and ourselves are changes in content and do not address the drift—the context. They help us improve what we are already practicing within the existing context. We throw more money at the issue, we restructure the organization, and we spend billions on self-help workshops, organizational training programs, or the "management theory du jour" and then wonder why the impact has been minimal. We forget that most skills and processes get their power from the context in which they are used. When these solutions are implemented within the drift, their impact is limited. For the most part these traditional solutions are like painting over rust—they look good at first, but they don't last.

When we operate from a familiar context, solutions for change come from what we already know. When those solutions fail to produce the results we want, we work harder at the solution, we try to get better at the solution, or we try some variation of the same solution. We fulfill Rita Mae Brown's definition of insanity: Doing the same thing over and over again and expecting a different result. At times it seems we are addicted to what is not working.

## ACCEPTING THE DRIFT FOR WHAT IT IS

As Fritjof Capra (1975, 23) wrote in *The Tao of Physics*, "the mechanistic worldview has been beneficial and detrimental at the same time. It was extremely successful in the development of classical physics and technology, but had many adverse consequences for our civilization." Likewise, it is not that these characteristics of the drift are bad or wrong. For most of us, living in the drift is the only way to be and it has served us well up to a point. However, the current drift is outdated, counterproductive, and contrary to our needs. It is, quite simply, detrimental to the personal satisfaction, family cooperation, and organizational productivity that we desire. Substantial and sustainable change will only come from intervening in the drift and creating a new context for ourselves. Are you willing for your relationships to work at a level beyond the drift? Are you willing to experience exhilarating satisfaction in your relationships? Are you willing to give up what you already know and experience a new level of excellence in relating to others and the results you produce? If so, you are ready to learn the principles of true partnership.

# 2 THE PRINCIPLES OF
## TRUE PARTNERSHIP

*We have it in our power to begin the world anew.*
—Thomas Paine

---

Once we shift the way we observe the world from the drift to one of true partnership, we actually experience greater power; not power in the familiar sense as in power over someone else, but in a more personal sense as in the power to accomplish. In mastering this power we gain capacities to think and act outside our normal limitations and develop the ability to generate extraordinary results for our organizations, our families, and ourselves.

---

IN 1961 PRESIDENT JOHN F. KENNEDY TOLD CONGRESS: "This nation should commit itself to achieving the goal, before this decade is out, of landing a man on the moon and returning him safely to earth." By making this bold declaration Kennedy created a new context. He intervened in traditional thinking where previous attempts at space travel had failed and its feasibility had been questioned.

We too can do the same. We can intervene in the drift that shapes our lives. To effectively intervene in the drift requires two things. First of all, we need to create and learn to articulate a new context. Second, we must develop a structure of new practices to support the new context. Kennedy's declaration to Congress forged a new context of space travel, but he also had to commit the funds and develop support structures such as NASA to make it viable. The same is true for us as individuals, families, or organizations.

During the twentieth century, revolutionary insights in the realm of science caused many people to question the fundamental premises on which the science of physics was based, the Newtonian mechanical model. The ideas that shaped this thinking—quantum theory—were so shocking that Einstein (1879–1955) wrote in his autobiography (1988, 45), "It was as if the ground had been pulled out from under one, with no firm foundation to be seen anywhere, upon which one could have built."

Quantum theory fundamentally altered the perception that all of matter was made up of individual particles. One of its most revolutionary ideas is called the "wave–particle duality." This theory states that matter is both particlelike and wavelike at the same time: the particle characteristics represent its individuality, and the wave characteristics its relatedness. Therefore, an object cannot be seen as an isolated entity but has to be understood through its relationships with the whole: "Quantum theory forces us to see the universe not as a collection of physical objects, but rather as a complicated web of relationships between the various parts of a unified whole" (Capra 1996, 30).

Another significant advance is that of the role of the observer. In the Newtonian world the observer simply witnesses reality as an external entity. In other words, there is no relationship between the observer and what is observed. In the quantum realm, however, the observer plays a critical role in perceiving reality. In fact, the observer's expectations can physically alter what is seen. In a classic experiment fundamental to quantum theory, it is proven that if physicists look for and measure characteristics of a particle they will see a particle, and if they look for and measure wave characteristics they will see wave patterns.

In the last seventy years quantum thinking revolutionized physics and then other sciences. It is now fundamental to most scientific practices and has provided major technological breakthroughs. Yet its application has not spilled over to alter our consciousness in other areas of our lives.

Just as the fundamental principles of Newtonian thinking have shaped our relationships until now, the profound insights of the new physics and quantum thinking provide a dramatically new context for our relationships. The new model of our physical world is based on principles of interconnectedness, a systems or holistic viewpoint, both–and thinking, and multiple possibilities. While the fundamentals of quantum physics challenge the way we observe the world and the connections between us, quantum thinking offers valuable new insights about the way we relate to one another and the results we produce when working together. A new world of quantum physics holism has replaced the familiar Newtonian emphasis on separate parts: "The quantum world has demolished the concept of the unconnected individual" (Wheatley 1992, 38).

The shift from Newtonian to quantum thinking is a shift from seeing a world made up of things to seeing the world as made up of relationships. Yet in this world of relatedness we don't lose our individuality. In the either–or thinking of the traditional Newtonian model, most people believe they must choose either the individual or the group. That is, to be a member of a team, you must lose your individuality; you must downplay your needs for the good of the group. As a result, most teams don't allow for the superstar performance of an individual.

Consider the possibility that being an individual does not mean being separate. In true partnership we can foster the conditions that access the potential of both the individual and the group. "The wave/particle dualism of quantum thinking offers a powerful model for seeing ourselves both as individuals, distinct and precious and effective in our own right, and at the same time as members of wider groups through which we acquire further identity and a wider capacity for relationship" (Zohar and Marshall 1994, 326).

This is one of the fundamental differences between superficial, or cosmetic, partnership and true partnership. Superficial partnership is a relationship where two distinct and different things (individuals) work toward a common goal, but not much else is changed. True partnership means the connection between the two individuals is fundamentally altered and that they actually co-evolve to a new level of relatedness.

As we change the context, we are able to move beyond the drift and create new opportunities. When we upgrade the quality of our relationships, individual satisfaction, family cooperation, and organizational effectiveness improve.

## True Partnership Is a New Context

True partnership represents as significant a shift in our relationships as quantum thinking did in the arena of physics. Niels Bohr, physicist and early proponent of quantum theory, once admitted, "If you aren't confused by quantum physics, then you haven't understood it" (as cited in Brian 1996, 177). The same could be said about true partnership. It is a new context—a new way of seeing people, situations, and events that is counterintuitive to everything we have learned. True partnership is not about using a few new buzzwords or following a standard recipe. It requires that we profoundly alter our connection with others.

True partnership means to shift from seeing other people as objects that can be molded and manipulated to seeing people as human beings with whom we are already connected and related. This is fundamental. This is the punch line. This is what it is all about. "The other person is not seen as someone who either takes power from us or is controlled by us at his or her expense, but as a companion in an evolving system" (Montuori and Conti 1993, 105).

A friend of mine told me a story at dinner recently that provides a simple but great example of how this connectedness can show up. It seems he was in a hurry to get to a meeting earlier that day and got behind a very slow driver on the highway. He tried honking and flipping his lights on and off, tried to change lanes to pass and, he was embarrassed to say, tried riding the bumper of the other car to get the driver to hurry up. He saw the other driver simply as an object in his path, and he tried to manipulate the other driver's behavior to get his own needs met. As he finally pulled alongside the car to pass it, he looked over to give one final glare. To his surprise, he saw his neighbor looking back at him. Immediately he was embarrassed and wanted to find a way to hide. Once we recognize we are already connected and related to others, we no longer see them as objects, and the quality of the relationship becomes more important.

True partnership is not instinctive. In fact, much of this information will seem counterintuitive to you. Most of us did not grow up in an environment that taught us the principles of true partnership. However, we can learn to move beyond the familiar and habitual we–they orientation, the inherent blame in prevalent thinking, the need to control and mold other people's behavior, the debating over who is right and who is wrong, and the fixed view of he/she/it. When we step outside the usual thinking and practices of power and control, we are no longer prisoners of a past that we have inherited from others.

True partnership must be generated. To have highly successful relationships, you must get out of the drift. By definition, this requires each of us to take the initiative to create a new context. In every interaction we must either generate a new quality to the communication or remain inside the drift. Granted, we cannot create a partnership alone, but we are the source of true partnership.

Listen to almost any conversation where someone is having a tough time with another person in his or her life and you will almost always hear strategies discussed about how the person should deal with the problem. Most strategies for change and attempts to improve relationships typically come from the drift—some variation of power and control: "What can I do to get them to do what I want them to do?" Strategies developed from the drift, build on the drift. True partnership is not a strategy for improvement.

True partnership is not something we do at certain times with certain people; it is a way of being. It is not a hat we put on when we go to the office in order to be more effective and then take off when we go home. True partnership is a way of looking at the people and the events in our lives that is with us all of the time. It permanently changes the way we perceive our world. When we read a paper or magazine, watch a movie or TV show, or watch interactions between people at home and at work, we will see different things. We will not focus on and judge the individual as right or wrong. We will, however, observe different patterns in the interactions between people and discover new solutions to problems in those interactions.

True partnership is not a position. When you or I take a position, we are saying it is right—making other positions wrong. One of the worst things graduates of our programs do is to leave the course with the arrogant idea that true partnership is right and the drift is wrong. This creates resistance because it is using the power and control model to condemn the power and control model. True partnership is a different context, one that gives you the ability to resolve current issues and create new opportunities that support your life more effectively than the power and control context.

True partnership is not the *right* way to be. It does not invalidate the drift. Einstein once compared a paradigm shift to climbing a mountain: The higher you go, the more you can see. The perspective from the top of the mountain is much broader and you can see more, yet it does not invalidate the views from lower parts of the mountain. When Copernicus proved the sun to be the center of the universe, I originally thought that invalidated the theory that the earth was the center of the universe. It took me a while to realize that prior to Copernicus the earth *was* the center of the universe. Only with new data and a more expansive perspective—a view from higher up the mountain—were people able to see differently.

The shift from a context of the drift to one of true partnership is not an either–or situation, which we could diagram like this.

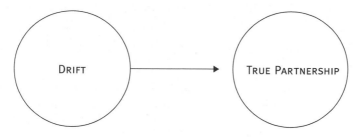

Rather, it is more like concentric circles, which can be represented this way.

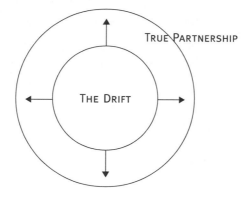

The perspective of true partnership includes the perspective of the drift. It does not make it wrong or invalidate it. True partnership simply provides a different, more expansive view. You can see things from true partnership that you cannot see from the drift.

True partnership is not some *nicey-nice* way of being more charming to get people to do what you want them to do. It sometimes entails being in each other's face. Many years ago when I was managing a hotel in St. Louis, I got a call that the local fire department was in the hotel on an inspection and was ready to shut us down for having too many banquet tables and chairs stored in a back hallway, blocking a fire exit. By the time I got to the back hallway, the assistant general manager was already there. This problem had been an ongoing issue, and today we had both had enough. We had a rather loud and very straight conversation with each other about the problem and how to get it permanently resolved. An hour later he was in my office and we were laughing together at how the employees around us had turned pale and looked for places to hide when seeing their two bosses upset with each other. Inside of our relationship, one of true partnership, we could talk like that to each other and not damage the relationship or carry over any resentment. That would not be so if we operated from the drift in our relationship. We also made sure that the people who witnessed that situation knew that our relationship was okay so rumors and gossip did not circulate.

Furthermore, just because you come from a context of true partnership does not guarantee you a perfect marriage or that you will always close a deal with prospective buyers or have perfect relationships with your boss or co-workers. People still break up, and managers still may have to let someone go. But when you come from a true partnership perspective, you have options for dealing with people that leave both of you whole and complete with no leftover anger and resentment.

## FOUR PRINCIPLES OF TRUE PARTNERSHIP

By using the principles of the new quantum paradigm in physics, we are able to create a new model for our relatedness to others. Let's now examine the principles that form the framework of the new context: connecting, communicating, expanding, and observing.

- *Connecting: We see ourselves as interdependent individuals, connected to one another as integral parts of a system.* Despite our habit of seeing ourselves as separate and autonomous, we actually live in an interdependent world. Interdependence generally means relying on each other to accomplish objectives. It also means that the success of the relationship depends on the success of the individual, and the success of the individual depends on the success of the relationship. Interdependence represents a shift from a "me equals results" to a "we equals results" attitude and gives us access to accomplishments that we, as individuals, cannot produce alone. The customary "I can do it on my own" approach just doesn't work in an interdependent world. Instead, in true partnership we begin to ask ourselves, "*What can we accomplish together?*"

- *Communicating: We connect to others through communication.* In true partnership the relationship, or connection, is emphasized rather than the individuals themselves. To come from true partnership means we see the value of a profound connection to others and constantly look for ways to improve this connection through our speaking and listening. We realize that there are things we can do to build a stronger relationship no matter what the other person does. In this manner, the people might not need to change, but the relationship can. We then recognize that perhaps we generate true partnership through communication and actions, both of which we are one hundred percent responsible for. Rather than being stuck in the drift, "There must be a way I can get them to do what I want them to do," it is more effective from a true partnership perspective to look at "*What is missing in the communication that might have an impact on the interaction?*"

- *Expanding: We operate from a both–and orientation.* One of the strengths of operating from true partnership is that it provides access to different perceptions about every situation. In true partnership we move beyond the polarizing effects of right–wrong and look for a unifying context that includes differing and perhaps even conflicting points of view. True partnership represents expanding viewpoints. This does not mean integrating into a common voice or diluting viewpoints to arrive at agreement. It does mean that all viewpoints have a right to be heard and that in true partnership one point of view does not have supremacy over another. Instead of coming from "There is a right way to do this, and it is usually my way," inherent in the conventional approach, we operate from true partnership and look at *What am I willing to learn in this interaction?"*

- *Observing: We relate to our world as observer-created.* Most of us think that what we see is fixed, independent of ourselves as the observer. There is a world "out there," and we are merely witnessing it. This is inconsistent with the principles of the new science. One of the fundamentals of quantum thinking is that reality emerges from our observations and the decisions or interpretations that we make about what we see. The decisions we make or the interpretations we apply are made from who we are, through the lens of our own personal history. Conflict between people is not so much about reality as it is about conflicting interpretations of reality. When we move beyond the typical "that's just the way it is thinking" to "that's the way it seems to be from my point of view," the world appears less rigid. We have more power in the situation or the circumstances, and we can open the door to new possibilities. We are freed up to then ask ourselves, *"What is another way I can view him/her/it?"*

These four principles become the structure to support the new context. They become the framework for new ways of seeing, thinking, and behaving.

People learning to master the principles of true partnership create a different world for themselves—a world full of possibilities. It is not utopia, nirvana, or heaven on earth but rather another way of seeing, a new context. It defines a new playing field. On that new playing field people, things, events, and processes can show up in totally new ways. "The whole of quantum reality is in fact a vast sea of potential" (Zohar and Marshall 1994, 46).

## THE IMPACT OF THE CONTEXT OF TRUE PARTNERSHIP

Because it is a new way of seeing, a new perspective, the context of true partnership will have a tremendous impact on all aspects of our relationships. Let's examine how some relationships appear differently in the drift and in true partnership.

### MANAGING

| IN THE DRIFT | IN TRUE PARTNERSHIP |
|---|---|
| The manager is seen as the boss who gives orders that others must follow. | The manager is seen as a facilitator of group efforts and ultimately accountable for the results of the group. |
| One-way, top-down communication is the norm. | Communication is a two-way process based on honesty. |
| The manager stands apart so as to not befriend the employees. | The manager relates to all members as equal human beings. |
| Information is kept close to the vest and not shared openly. | Information is shared openly so everyone knows the score. |
| The manager's job is to motivate employees to maximize performance and to use strategies such as incentive plans or disciplinary procedures to get the job done. | The manager's job is to provide an environment for motivated people to excel and all people are seen as having a basic motivation to succeed. |
| Managers evaluate the performance of their subordinates. | The manager and each member evaluates each other's performance as to how they contributed to the partnership and the results. |
| Unilateral decision making by a few people is followed by attempts to get buy-in from others. | Ownership is created by giving those people affected by a particular decision an opportunity to express their agenda in the decision-making process. |

## SELLING

### IN THE DRIFT

Selling is seen as the process of getting the buyer to purchase your product or service by whatever means possible.

Buyers are seen as malleable, controllable, and able to be manipulated if only the seller finds the right gimmick or message.

Seller wants to use information about the buyer or techniques to get them to reach a decision already determined by the seller.

A sales process of opening, probing, presenting, handling objections, and closing is used.

When the buyer does not buy, there is something the salesperson could have or should have done differently to close the sale.

### IN TRUE PARTNERSHIP

Selling is seen as a process of helping buyers find solutions or make decisions that are the most appropriate for them.

Buyers are seen as self-directing and capable of assuming responsibility for their own decisions.

The seller wants to help the buyer reach a decision of the buyer's own choosing based on the buyer's needs and wants.

Selling is a process of facilitating the buyer through the steps of the decision-making process.

The only thing a seller can do, or should do, is to help the buyer make the best decision.

## COACHING

### IN THE DRIFT

The coach is seen as someone who is wiser and has more experience and tells the player what to do to be successful.

Coaching is viewed as giving advice and is authoritative and directive.

The coach uses rewards and punishment to improve performance.

### IN TRUE PARTNERSHIP

A coach is seen as someone who has a different point of view that, when communicated effectively, may enable the player to see actions he or she could not see before that will lead to different results.

Coaching is supportive and provides guidance to where the individual wants to be.

The coach recognizes that the player has the fundamental capabilities to accomplish the objectives but may need support in getting there.

| | |
|---|---|
| The goal of coaching is to improve performance at any cost. | The goal of coaching is to create an atmosphere of growth and development while accomplishing the goals. |
| The coach or organization develops the objectives. | The coach or organization and the player create and build a shared vision. |

## TEAMWORK

| IN THE DRIFT | IN TRUE PARTNERSHIP |
|---|---|
| The team is seen as a group of individuals who must be managed in order to maximize performance. | The team is viewed as a web of relationships that can be enhanced to maximize performance. |
| Individuals are ostracized if they don't perform. | Individuals are supported through straight talk to improve performance. |
| Agreement and conformity are valued, and members are nice to each other while hiding their true thoughts and feelings. | Self-expression is encouraged as a contribution to the group. |
| Confrontations are avoided because they may upset the "harmony" of the team. | People actively confront and resolve issues. |
| Problems are handled privately by management. | Problems are handled by the team, as a group, in open conversation. |
| The team relates to one another through their judgments and opinions about each other. | The team relates to one another through their mutual commitments. |

## PARENTING

| IN THE DRIFT | IN TRUE PARTNERSHIP |
|---|---|
| Parents are seen as having a particular agenda and are responsible for managing a child's progress toward that end. | Parents are seen as having the ability to see the child's viewpoint and to encourage the child to grow as a healthy, self-directing human being. |
| Parents direct the child along a certain path to avoid pitfalls and mistakes. | Parents support the child through the growing years, treating pitfalls and mistakes as learning experiences. |

## PARENTING *(continued)*

| In the Drift | In True Partnership |
|---|---|
| Parents are seen as being responsible for molding the child's behavior through rewards and punishment. | Parents are seen as being responsible for supporting the development of the child through compassionate listening and authentic straight talk. |
| Parents are seen as teachers who give advice based on their own experience, wisdom, and maturity. | Parents challenge and encourage growth by making alternative points of view for exploration available. |

## CONFLICT RESOLUTION

| In the Drift | In True Partnership |
|---|---|
| Conflict is seen as destructive, something to avoid like a disease that must be eradicated. | Conflict is seen as productive, an opportunity to remove obstacles in relationships, and is considered to be an essential ingredient of a healthy relationship. |
| Conflict is a disagreement, a power struggle that has only winners and losers. | Conflict is a conversation where everybody wins. |
| Conflict is uncomfortable for most people and is generally swept under the carpet. | Conflict provides an opportunity to facilitate change and growth for both the individuals and the relationship. |

When we shift the way we view the world from a model based on power and control to one grounded in the principles of true partnership, people, situations, and events in our world show up differently. We begin to see things we could not see before, we relate to people in new ways, we address problems differently, and we discover new solutions to existing issues.

Several years ago, shortly after I began my exploration of partnership, I was amazed at what happened when I had an opportunity to "walk the talk" of this work. I had been doing some volunteer work with the executive team of a nonprofit group. At this particular meeting I was asked to co-chair a very important committee with Ellen, who was one of the other members of the executive team. This did not make me happy. I had not had positive experiences working with Ellen in the past, and this project was very important to the future of the group. I thought Ellen was too pushy, arrogant, and egotistical for this assignment, and it seemed to me that she became very moody if she wasn't in control. I was concerned about the success of this sensitive project if she were involved.

The next day I was talking with a close friend and shared my concerns. She listened for a while and then said something that literally rocked my world. Knowing well my work in the arena of partnership, she asked me, "What would it be like if you looked at Ellen as your partner in this project?" Well, at first I was taken aback, then embarrassed. Then I replied, "You mean put the principles of partnership into action? What a novel idea." So I did just that. I let go of my judgments of Ellen and decided to see her as my partner. Instead of seeing her as an object that would inhibit me, I focused on the quality of the relationship between us. That opened the door to a new way of relating to Ellen.

That conversation made a significant contribution to my life and my work. It really drove home the power of context and how we observe the world. It seemed to me that Ellen had really changed by the time of our next meeting, but what had changed was *my perception*. Our work together on that committee was amazing. We accomplished more than any of us thought possible, and I developed a tremendous admiration for Ellen and her commitment to this particular nonprofit group. I was astonished at the outcome of applying these principles of true partnership to my own actions.

After sharing this same story in our workshops, many people would ask me, "But how did you do it? How do you change your perception?" My first response was always, "You just do it!" More recently I have seen that there is more to it than that. To change our perceptions, we must change our focus, or more accurately, we must change what we are focusing on. As I sit here in my office, I can create a totally different perception and different feelings if I change my focus from what is out of place or wasn't dusted properly to the artwork on the walls, the pictures of my children and grandchildren, or the antique lamp that my fiancée gave me.

The same is true in our relationships. Rather than focusing on our self or our judgments about the other person, when we focus on the relationship and put practices in place to improve the relationship, we shift the entire context.

Here is another example to reinforce this point. A friend of mine in real estate was talking recently about her broker, Dave. It seems that my friend was having a great deal of difficulty relating to Dave and never felt comfortable in conversations with him. She said he was "emotionally unavailable" and that he was too dry and would not loosen up. I reviewed with her the true partnership perspective, and she agreed to give it a try.

The next day she called and was overjoyed. Evidently, she decided to give up her focus on Dave and her judgments about him and concentrate on the relationship—the quality of the connection between them. After the sales meeting that morning she went into Dave's office and began a conversation. During the conversation she asked him for his thoughts on a few items, and before she knew it they were in a great discussion about the pros and cons of real estate. Dave even spent a great deal of time sharing his own frustrations with the organization and some of his personal goals and objectives for the coming year. My friend was both shocked and delighted. She couldn't understand how a simple change of focus could create such an extraordinary change in their working relationship. She personally experienced the value of true partnership and how she had generated it on her own.

Only when you transform the way you view someone or something can you generate any significant change. Until that time, all attempts to alter the situation will have little if any impact.

For many years in our sales training program I taught a segment on listening, and I personally saw the power of context. At that time most salespeople thought of selling as a chess game—applying a series of strategies to corner the buyer and get him or her to buy. These salespeople would use their new listening skills as a way to get information from the buyer to load their presentation gun with ammunition to fire back at the buyer. Only when salespeople changed their viewpoint about selling to assisting the buyer in accomplishing what he or she needed did the application of the listening skills have a real impact. They then saw listening as an opportunity to get into the buyer's world and truly understand his or her viewpoint so they could help the buyer reach an appropriate buying decision. Same skills, different application, and remarkably different results.

A true partnership perspective provides each of us with an opportunity for personal transformation that promises to improve the quality of our relationships—and our lives. "We cannot leave the selection of the next step in the evolution of human society and culture to chance. We must plan for it, consciously and purposefully" (Laszlo 1985, 16).

# 3 Connecting: The Interdependent Nature of Life

*The reality can no longer be ignored that we live in an interdependent world which is bound together by a common destiny.* —Nelson Mandela

---

Despite our habit of seeing ourselves as separate and autonomous, we are actually connected to each other through our relationships. We live in an interdependent world. Interdependence represents a shift from a "me equals results" to a "we equals results" attitude and gives us access to things we cannot accomplish alone. The customary "I can do it on my own" approach allows for limited success in an interdependent, interconnected world. In true partnership we ask ourselves, "What can we accomplish together?"

---

THE FIRST PRINCIPLE OF TRUE PARTNERSHIP is connecting. We see ourselves as interdependent individuals, connected to one another as integral parts of a system. This principle reflects the new emphasis on unity and integration in the world of quantum physics. In the Newtonian paradigm of physics, all reality is fragmented into basic parts (atoms). Each part seems inherently separate from every other part and connected to others only externally. Like billiard balls colliding on a pool table, these separate parts meet and go their separate ways.

The fundamental wave–particle duality of quantum physics shows us a different view of reality wherein the particle aspect of matter tends to stay separate and the wave aspects merge and overlap. Thus, in the quantum paradigm the world is seen not as a collection of separate objects but as a network of entities that are fundamentally interconnected and, therefore, interdependent. So instead of the "I can do it on my own" thinking inherent in the traditional approach to relationships, we begin with a *"What can we accomplish together?"* orientation in true partnership.

The power of this concept can be seen in the history of the development of the computer. Originally computers were stand-alone machines, and they were capable of producing more than we had ever thought possible. However, this was nowhere near what is possible today—now that we have connected computers through networks. We now know that the real power of computers comes from the connections between them. The same is true for humans.

Most of us generally think of interdependence as the relationship between two people or entities where each is dependent on the other. For example, you and I would have an interdependent relationship if we were climbing a mountain roped together. Either we both get to the top or neither of us does. If you fall off the side of the mountain, it would not do any good for me to say "It's your fault" as we fall to the ground together.

There seems to be a typical growth pattern for most of us from dependent to independent. We are born dependent on our parents for food and other survival necessities. Life then becomes a quest for independence. Our greatest accomplishments come from those situations where we seem to prove our independence. We are praised when we become potty trained, learn to tie our own shoes, and when we can recite the alphabet. Later in life we are praised when we learn to drive a car, get our first job, graduate from college, or move out on our own. Our independence—"I can do it on my own" thinking—is our primary objective.

Independence is not a high enough goal for mature, healthy people. To be able to make it on our own is a view of life focused directly on the self. Interdependence is the next step in our evolution. It fulfills one of the most basic of human needs—the desire to make a difference in the lives of others and for our life to mean something. This can only be developed through our interconnectedness, our relationships to each other.

What if interdependence also involved the idea that there is something I can contribute to the quality of the relationship and therefore the other person, so each of us, as individuals, becomes stronger as a result of the connection, the relationship? Think of the positive cycle this would initiate. The enhanced quality of the relationship enables each member to feel stronger and therefore able to contribute more to the relationship. As the relationship becomes stronger, the members become stronger. This is what is really possible in true partnership.

## YOUR NETWORK OF RELATIONSHIPS

To examine the interdependent nature of your life, complete this diagram by asking yourself, "Who do I have a relationship with that affects the quality of my life?" In other words, identify all those people with whom you interact in the everyday process of life.

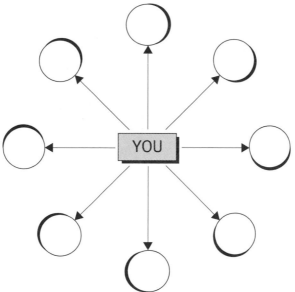

Here are some people you might include on your list:

| | |
|---|---|
| spouse/partner | ex-spouse |
| children | neighbors |
| parents/siblings | teachers |
| in-laws | banker |
| friends | religious/spiritual leader |
| boss | senior management |
| clients and customers | vendors/suppliers |
| support people | board of directors |
| people from other departments | people from outside agencies |
| peers and co-workers | volunteer group members |

We interact with a great many people each day. These people have an impact on the quality of our lives and on our ability to get done what we need to get done—at home and at work. Being aware of the importance of all your interactions will give you access to greater success in a paradigm of interdependence. Visualize your network of relationships as you think about these key points.

- Our joy, happiness, satisfaction, effectiveness, and sense of well-being lie in our relationships. Likewise our sense of frustration when things don't get done when we need them to be done resides in our relationship network. Many of us report at the end of the day, "I could have accomplished more today if only so-and-so had done such-and-such."

- No matter how capable you or I might be, we are nothing without an effective and workable relationship network. Even if you become a famous individual, the quality of your life would not change unless the quality of your relationships changed also. We can't have a great life without great relationships. Ultimately the quality of our lives is a function of our relatedness.

- You and I define ourselves through our relationships. Our personalities, our values, and our objectives in life are all shaped by our relatedness to others.

- There is a great deal of diversity. Each of these people and groups of people have different agendas and diverse viewpoints. They have their own unique way of looking at the world, going about doing their job, and living their lives. Conflicts often arise from the different agendas and viewpoints. These conflicts, if not resolved effectively, damage the communication, the outcomes of our interactions, and the quality of the relationship.

- We spend a lot of time and energy trying to change others. We develop strategies and approaches to get them to do what we want. We think we can mold people into being what we want them to be, and we keep looking for the magical solution.

- Most of our work and effort to get people to change is to no avail. People resist our efforts to change them. All that really needs to change to create different outcomes is the quality of the connection, the communication between us.

- Notice that you are in the middle. Most of us have a great deal more influence in our relationships than we might think. When the relationship is not working, it is easier to blame the circumstances or the other person or, in some cases, ourselves, than to look at how to communicate differently. It could be said that our relationship network is a mirror image of our own beliefs. So when things don't work out, the first place to look is within, but not with blame or guilt. Look at what you could do differently. What are your judgments and evaluations of the other person? How are you listening or not listening to them? What is it that you are not saying that keeps your resentment alive?

## ESSENTIAL ELEMENTS OF CONNECTING

What does it mean when we say that in true partnership we see ourselves as interdependent individuals connected to one another as integral parts of a system? Ask yourself, "What can I do to live this principle on a daily basis?" Two essential elements may shed some light on this issue for you:

- Focus on the connection, the relationship, not the individuals.
- Build accountability into the relationship by concentrating on "us" rather than on "we–they."

### Focus on the Connection

Focus on the connection, the relationship, not the individuals. In the drift, two people, a family, a team of people, or an organization is seen as a collection of individuals. Granted they interact with one another so there are relationships between and among them, but the relationships are secondary. In quantum thinking, the true partnership context, the relationships are primary.

Typically in relating to others we tend to focus on the individual. We notice the other person's age, gender, appearance, weight, race, and many other things and compare what we see to ourselves or to some social norm: Who is better off? Who is not? This automatic, and for many people unconscious, judging has a significant impact on our relationships. We quickly determine whether we like them, or whether or not they like us. We get very good at sizing people up, and it is a fact of life that the first several seconds in an interaction make a significant impact on how we relate to one another.

We have even gotten so sophisticated as to categorize each other by personality types. Organizations spend millions of dollars annually on personality profiling. I think you know what I mean—the process of identifying the personality type or quadrant description that we assign to people. Please understand this before you read on—I am *not* criticizing this process. A lot of value comes from understanding our own personality characteristics and recognizing that everyone does not think or act as we do. There are, however, significant limitations when we label people and put them in a category, a box if you will, and then expect to build and maintain productive and satisfying relationships with them.

Communication problems between people are often discounted as personality conflicts. What a cop out! We are different, and we all have different values and different ways of getting things done. Everybody knows that. When people tell me they can't get things resolved because of a personality conflict, what I see is people stuck on being right and unable or unwilling to look at new solutions. "They have a personality conflict" has become an acceptable excuse, but this viewpoint means that no one has to be responsible for getting the problem resolved. Convenient for some, perhaps, but not productive.

The more we focus on the differences between people, the more we create separation. And most of us feel separate enough. We do not need to increase the distance between us. I once attended a seminar where the leader asked everyone who feels separate from the rest of the group to stand up. To our astonishment, everyone stood up. He then asked for some of the reasons we felt separate and listed them on the blackboard. It was utterly amazing. The list included some of the more obvious physical things: "I'm older," "I'm heavier," "I'm not as good looking," "My nose is too big," or "I don't dress as nice." But it also included things you couldn't even tell about others such as "I'm not as smart," "I'm not as rich," "I am more financially well-off," "I don't have a retirement account," "I grew up with an alcoholic mother," "I was abused as a child," or "I owe money to the IRS." The point is that *everyone* has something about himself or herself that keeps us separate from others.

In the interdependent world of today the sense of being separate is very limiting. We must learn to enhance the connection, the relationship between us. Quantum physics introduced the concept of "systems thinking." Fundamentally, a system has come to mean "an integrated whole whose essential properties arise from the relationship between the parts" (Capra 1996, 27). So, a system—such as true partnership—arises out of the connection between the parts. The quality of the connection between us, the parts, is determined by many variables including the empathy of the listening, the authenticity of the speaking, the frequency of the interactions, the richness of the communication, and the things we find we have in common.

Therefore, to improve a relationship it behooves us to look not at how the other person needs to change or how we need to change but at how the *quality of the connection* can shift. How can we listen more effectively, speak more authentically, be in communication more frequently, have richer communication, and find things we have in common? In actuality, this may be the only thing we have real control over after all. The bottom line: It has nothing to do with who we think the other person is or what we think they think about us, the effectiveness of the system is shaped by the quality of the relationship. So why not focus on what really matters?

## Build Accountability

Build accountability into the relationship by concentrating on "us" rather than "we–they." Just as soon as we separate ourselves from others, we set up a we–they orientation, which reinforces our separateness everywhere in our lives. At home we–they shows up in many ways such as parent–child, man–woman, and young–old. At work this duality is found in management–employees, sales–operations, home office–field, old timers–new people, and boss–subordinates. The tendency is to build walls between the others and ourselves and to defend or protect our particular position. And, as soon as we set up we–they, we introduce the component of blame.

Relationships, families, teams, and organizations are all crippled by blame. At home we blame our parents, our spouse, or the kids. At work, we blame the culture, the customer, the boss, or the other department. Finger-pointing and blame seem to be the norm rather than the exception. Whether spoken or not, blame is in the background of many conversations. Who is wrong, who made the mistake, and who should apologize dominate our relationships. What if more people were accountable for their behavior?

I recently worked with the five regional sales managers of a client company. To make things easier for their paper flow, they requested that I invoice each of the five regions separately. I agreed with the stipulation that the invoices would be paid within ten days and that I would not have to follow up on the five different invoices. They assured me it would not be a problem. One invoice was paid in ten days, two others in twenty-one days. The final two invoices took several phone calls and were not paid for over a month. In those cases, the regional manager said he had processed the invoice properly but that the accounting department had screwed up. Since all five regions processed their invoices through a central accounting office and one invoice had been paid on time, I decided to investigate the situation. I was sure there was something of value for the company to learn here. As it turned out, only one regional manager had processed the invoice promptly—the invoice that was paid in ten days as agreed. Two managers took a couple of weeks to approve the invoices, and the other two almost a month. In each case the accounting office took only four to five days to cut a check and process the payment, and you should have heard how much that office was blamed for my not receiving payment on time.

When we move to us, meaning we are in this together, we are able to move beyond blame to relationships where accountability exists. True partnership represents a context where two people are not different entities with different agendas or working in different directions (we–they) but two people who work together and form a new entity (us) that displays cohesiveness and connectedness. When you and I come from a true partnership perspective we, by definition, take on being accountable for the quality of the relationship.

For example, if my relationship with one of my grown children is not what I want it to be, it would be easy (when operating from the drift) to blame them. They haven't returned my calls, or they don't share what's going on in their lives with me. On the other hand, when coming from true partnership, seeing the relationship from us, I become accountable for what's not working and look to what I can do to improve the relationship. Then, when I am not so busy blaming, I can see new actions to take. For example, I could initiate the calls or a conversation about what is missing for me and what we can do about it.

## Connecting in Action

Rick was general sales manager for a global telecommunication company. He was based in Los Angeles and his eleven-person leadership team was responsible for more than $230 million in sales and more than 120 employees. The leadership team was broken down into two fairly distinct geographic and cultural groups. One group, responsible for San Diego and Orange Counties, was based in Orange County and seemed to be more conservative, stable, and reserved. The other group, responsible for Los Angeles and based in Los Angeles, seemed to be more hard-edged, prone to take risks, and less trusting.

From Rick's point of view, the largest issue facing the team was the lack of trust for the "other camp." In addition to this issue, recognition and compensation were tied to individual results. It was incumbent upon the managers to protect their people and their turf, oftentimes to the detriment of their peers and the entire regional team. Furthermore, due to pressure from the company, there was a real sense of urgency to deliver short-term sales results.

The leadership team participated in our partnership courses. By utilizing the principles and practices of true partnership, they created a real sense of camaraderie on the team. Not only were they more open to each other's views and needs, but also to the views and needs of their extended teams, who they dealt with on a daily basis. While the team gained awareness and specific skills such as empathic listening, authentic communication, and effective conflict resolution during the courses, the greatest impact was in the arena of team building. They moved beyond the we–they thinking inherent in the drift and recognized the value of an interdependent approach. Rick said, "The closeness and honesty among the team improved exponentially." Dealing with difficult issues in a kind and caring way became the norm. They emerged a stronger, better performing team as a direct result of the principles and practices of true partnership.

In true partnership, we move beyond acting as if we are separate and autonomous and the subsequent we–they thinking that limits performance and look for ways to create alignment and ensure the future of the system. When we realize the interdependent nature of our life, we look at how we can communicate differently to enhance the connection and therefore the results. We see ourselves as accountable for the results of the whole and are actually empowered to take actions that contribute to the relationship. "A self that fails to create itself as a contribution to others is irrelevant in a systems world. If our self expression is not meaningful to others we will not survive" (Wheatley and Kellner-Rogers 1996, 52).

When there is a breakdown in communication between people at home or at work and you hear we–they and blame, it is time to remember the principle of connecting in the true partnership context. Then, like Rick (the general sales manager in Los Angeles), we will

- realize the interdependent nature of life and that our success is dependent on the success of the others involved.
- focus on the relationship and look for ways to upgrade the quality of the connection.

- develop an "us" attitude and become accountable for the quality of the relationship.
- relate to others based on what they can contribute, not on their personalities or our judgments about them.

When we value connecting and see ourselves as interdependent parts of the whole, our organizations become

- more aligned toward common goals and objectives.
- more effective and able to react quickly in today's time-sensitive marketplace.
- less limited by the "silo" effect of we–they thinking.
- places where people are more willing to share resources and help each other.
- less focused on blame and more focused on what works.
- happier, healthier, and more productive.

In true partnership, you will find yourself focusing less on being separate and autonomous and instead ask yourself, "What can we accomplish together?" This message is driven home in this poem by James Patrick Kinney.

THE COLD WITHIN

Six humans trapped by happenstance
In bleak and bitter cold.
Each one possessed a stick of wood
Or so the story's told.

Their dying fire in need of logs
The first man held his back.
For of the faces round the fire,
He noticed one was black.

The next man looking cross the way
Saw one not of his church,
And couldn't bring himself to give
The fire his stick of birch.

The third one sat in tattered clothes
He gave his coat a hitch.
Why should his log be put to use
To warm the idle rich?

The rich man just sat back and thought
Of the wealth he had in store.
And how to keep what he had earned
From the lazy, shiftless poor.

The black man's face bespoke revenge
As the fire passed from his sight,
For all he saw in his stack of wood
Was a chance to spite the white.

The last man of this forlorn group
Did naught except for gain,
Giving only to those who gave
Was how he played the game.

Their logs held tight in death's still hand
Was proof of human sin.
They did not die from the cold without —
They died from the cold within.

There is real power in a strong connection between people where each wants to contribute to the other. When there is this kind of a connection, the "stuff" of the drift goes away. Most of us have felt this connection at one time or another. We call it chemistry. We have all met people in both our personal and professional lives where everything seemed to "click" right off the bat. True partnership is a way to consciously and purposefully create that kind of connection more frequently instead of waiting for it to magically appear.

# 4 COMMUNICATING: TRANSFORMING RELATIONSHIPS THROUGH SPEAKING AND LISTENING

*When people communicate, they don't simply pass information back and forth. They get things done, sharing interpretations and making commitments that change the status of their work, their world and their future.* —Fernando Flores

In true partnership the relationship—the connection—is emphasized rather than the individuals. The quality of the connection is shaped through communication, the primary building block of a relationship. To come from true partnership means we see the value of a profound connection to others and constantly look for ways to improve this connection through our speaking and listening. We realize that there are things we can do to build a stronger relationship, no matter what the other person does. People might not need to change, but the relationship always can. We then recognize that we generate true partnership by being one hundred percent responsible for our communication and actions.

IN THE TRADITIONAL NEWTONIAN MODEL, the particle is the fundamental building block of our world. Particles are connected to other particles through the forces of attraction and repulsion. As we have seen, in the quantum paradigm the focus shifts from particles to the relationship between the particles—a shift from "thingness" to "relatedness."

In the first principle of true partnership, connecting, we shift our focus from the individuals to the relationship between the individuals. The second principle of true partnership is that we connect to others through communication. Communication is the fundamental building block of relationships. How we speak and how we listen in each and every interaction with others shapes the quality of the relationship.

A relationship or organization consists of individuals with unique knowledge and talents, different backgrounds and levels of experience, and personal agendas and diverse viewpoints who rely on each other to get things done. Typically, in the normal process of living and working together, we talk a lot with each other—but there is very little effective communication. Communication is more than idle chitchat around the dinner table or the office water cooler. It is so much more than the exchange of information.

People do communicate a lot with each other in today's workplace, and we exchange a great deal of information. There seems to be an abundance of faxes, cell phones, pagers, emails, meetings, and memos. Technology makes it possible to communicate even more frequently, but most of this talk is not effective communication. More and more, we are simply talking at each other rather than *with* each other.

In true partnership, communication contributes to the nature of the relationship. Implied in this definition of communication is the fact that something happens as a result of the interaction—that is, things get done. Through effective communication we are able to get into each other's world and create a bond in the relationship that moves us beyond the limitations of the drift. True partnership calls for us to be aware of the power of our words and of how listening enhances the outcomes of our interactions. In this way we can then move beyond the thinking inherent in the paradigm of power and control, "There must be something I can do to get you to do what I want you to do," to asking ourselves, *"What is missing in the communication that might contribute to the outcome?"*

Communication continues to be the biggest obstacle to effective interpersonal relationships. Year in and year out, communication ranks as the biggest problem on most employee satisfaction surveys. Yet seldom do we see much emphasis placed on learning the fundamental skills of interpersonal communication: speaking and listening. Instead, we see many of the same old solutions to this problem—more top-down information thrown at employees thinking that this will finally solve the communication dilemma. In my work with clients, I have experienced many introductions of new strategies and initiatives designed to improve morale and organizational performance. And each year as technology improves, so does the pizzazz of the fabulous multimedia presentation designed to motivate the team to communicate better and produce more. But after the glitz of the presentation, after the carefully crafted speech of the president, and after the fantastic spread of delicious food, we go back to the same work environment. Typically this context is built on a foundation of ineffective communication where people do not listen, do not speak straight, and do not confront and resolve problems that inhibit their performance.

To live effectively in the context of true partnership, we must develop radically new practices around our communication with each other. Because the quality of the connection is determined by how we speak and how we listen, we must learn to listen at a totally new level and to speak straight in ways that contribute to the relationship. "To live in a quantum world . . . we will need to become savvy about how to build relationships, how to nurture growing, evolving things. All of us will need better skills in listening, communicating, and facilitating groups, because these are the talents that build strong relationships" (Wheatley 1992, 38).

## EFFECTIVE LISTENING: UNDERSTANDING
## ANOTHER'S PERSPECTIVE

Many people leave our workshops saying "I thought I was a good listener until I attended this program." For some reason many of us continue to operate with a grade school comprehension of what listening is and how to do it effectively. Instead of understanding what the speaker is saying, we give unwarranted advice, judge and evaluate the speaker, determine whether we agree with what the speaker is saying or not, and think about what to say next. As a result, we are unable to leave another person with a sense of being heard and understood. This is a vital ingredient of an effective relationship.

Even though much has been said and written about listening, it constantly amazes me how little most of us know about listening and, more important, how little we practice effective listening. My goal is to raise the bar about listening. I want us to move beyond the conventional definition of listening toward a deeper understanding. Effective listening is not a technique. I should know. I spent many years teaching it as a technique, and I can tell you that only those people who applied the skill in the appropriate context were successful.

I believe listening has a spiritual nature. Our capacity to listen enables us to connect with others on a deeper level. It opens the door to a profound sense of relatedness. When you or I truly listen to another human being, we move beyond simply hearing and reacting to the words and connect with the speaker's soul. We discover the speaker's inner world, the world that really matters to him or her. Listening actually accesses and brings out the potential of others. It is about understanding and validating that someone else's perspective of the world is the truth for them and is as legitimate and valid for them as our truth is for us. Carl Rogers (1980), in *A Way of Being*, describes listening at this level:

An empathic way of being with another person has several facets. It means entering the private perceptual world of another and being thoroughly at home with it. . . . It means temporarily living in another's life, moving about in it delicately without making judgments; it means sensing meanings of which he or she is scarcely aware, but not trying to uncover totally unconscious feelings, since this would be too threatening. . . . It means frequently checking with the other person as to the accuracy of your sensings, and being guided by the responses you receive (142).

There are three distinctions surrounding listening that we will examine. They do not include the basics of maintaining good eye contact and body posture, of being silent while the other person is speaking and not interrupting, and asking open-ended questions rather than closed questions to encourage greater conversation. These are the basics of listening that we should all know by now. Listening is far too critical a skill for us to stay at the level of the basics. Let's agree to move beyond the basics and challenge each other to new levels and new distinctions of listening to each other. The three distinctions that we will examine are these:

- Listening for clarity
- Listening for understanding
- Listening for partnership

## Listening for Clarity

We learned earlier how context shapes our experience. Context is the filter through which we see and listen to others. Listening for clarity means that we are aware of our filters and how they shape what we hear. To really listen to another and understand their world means that we will not be limited by the filters through which we listen. Here is an example that I have shared in workshops. I find it is true for both men and women, but I will share it from my own perspective.

Imagine that I am driving down the road and my passenger says "You can change lanes now," or as we are pulling into a parking lot, "There's a parking space." My initial reaction (not always spoken) used to be something like "Okay, okay, don't you think I can drive?" or "I'm not blind you know" or "She's being pushy and controlling." Whether I said anything or not, the hair would stand up on the back of my neck and my blood pressure would probably rise. Once I even pulled over to the side of the road and said "Here, do you want to drive?" Now, before you start thinking "Boy, this guy is really too sensitive," I want you to know that most people can relate to this example in some form—either as the driver or the passenger. The point is that my passenger said "There's a parking place over there" and I heard "I don't know what I'm doing."

Years later I finally got smart and asked, "What do you mean by that?" Many of you already know the answer. She replied, "I'm just trying to contribute." And I got it. Here she is in the passenger seat, probably bored to begin with because she's not driving. She sees a parking spot open up and merely wants to point it out. I'm driving and focusing on other cars, and she doesn't know if I see it or not. Wow! Pretty simple. Since that day, I have never had a problem in this situation. I simply changed my filter from "She's controlling me" to "She's contributing to me."

What we hear from another person is usually what we want to hear or what we have been conditioned to hear rather than what they said. Once we realize the impact our filters have on how we listen, we are able to listen to others with much greater clarity.

## Listening for Understanding

Accurately understanding the message is simply the first step in effective listening. The sender of the message, the other person, must feel heard and understood for the communication cycle to be complete. It is essential to stress that it is not for the receiver (the listener) to feel that he or she has understood the message but that the sender (the speaker) has a sense that the listener understood the message. It does not do any good to respond to the speaker by saying, "I understand what you are saying." Especially since the word "but" is probably the next word out of the listener's mouth. The listener must check in, must respond in some way that lets the sender know he or she has heard and accurately understood the communication.

The best way to accomplish this is through the skill of active listening. It is also referred to as reflective listening, paraphrasing, or the feedback loop. I am partial to the term active listening as it was developed by Dr. Thomas Gordon and taught in his books and courses, *Parent Effectiveness Training* (1977) and *Leader Effectiveness Training* (1977), and in the book he and I co-authored, *Sales Effectiveness Training* (1993).

In active listening the listener responds by paraphrasing back to the sender both the facts and the feelings that the listener has interpreted. "It is important to remember that all messages have two parts—the verbal (the words) and the nonverbal (voice tone, facial expression, or posture). Furthermore, most messages contain two types of information: the person's thoughts, ideas, knowledge or data (the facts), and the person's emotions, attitudes, sentiments, and values (the feelings) associated with those facts. The careful listener must tune in to both of these elements to achieve true understanding" (Zaiss and Gordon 1993, 79). Here are some examples of active listening:

> SENDER: Why can't you get things done like you promised?
>
> LISTENER: It seems to me that you're upset that we didn't get that information to you on time.

SENDER: I certainly don't want to rush in and make a decision that I'll be sorry for later.

LISTENER: You're really apprehensive about making the right decision.

SENDER: I just don't understand all of the fine print in that contract.

LISTENER: It sounds like you're really confused over all the little details.

Without mastering this skill of active listening, it is very difficult to sustain quality relationships. Likewise, without creating a context of true partnership to begin with, the skill of active listening loses much of its impact. In the wrong context, it can come across as trite and patronizing. Remember, skills get their power from the context in which they are used.

At the end of the first day in all of my workshops, I assign some homework. The assignment is to go home and use the active listening skill during a conversation. Typically at this point of the program participants are not yet proficient in the skill, but they are asked to try it anyway. The morning of the second day I begin by reviewing the homework, and this is one of the most enjoyable portions of leading the course. Even a novice's attempt to hear and understand others creates miracles in people's lives. The participants come in and typically report extraordinary conversations with spouses, children, and others. Many times participants are profoundly moved by what they experienced from doing this seemingly simple homework assignment.

## Listening for Partnership

In addition to listening to understand another's perspective, it is important to listen for the possibilities of partnership. In other words, to listen for what you and the speaker might accomplish together or have in common. What is the connection between you and the other person that can be used to move beyond the drift—the sense of being separate? This is what enables us to build a powerful connection and provide an opportunity for true partnership to grow.

As I said earlier, we all have filters that determine what we hear. Typically our filters are shaped by the traditional model of being separate and autonomous and connected by forces of power and control. So what we hear is how separate we are, and we listen for things that reinforce our separateness. If that's the case, why not consciously change the filter—like I did from "she's controlling" to "she's contributing"—to one of true partnership? We will hear words differently and perhaps discover new messages. Rather than differences, we will hear similarities and things we have in common on which to strengthen our connection.

After many years of facilitating workshops, this concept really struck home for me. I began to notice that in most groups a few people would dramatically improve their performance as a result of our work together. And, of course, there were a few that didn't get anything out of the workshop. I said the same thing to everyone in the room. Obviously what made a difference was how people listened. So I started beginning each workshop with a discussion about what I had seen. I began by saying, "Consider for a moment that nothing I say here has any value! What if the only thing of value is how you listen—are you listening to me as your partner or someone who is trying to change you?" Wow, that blew people away. They eventually got the point. As a partner in the classroom, they are responsible for what they learn during the workshop. It really made a significant contribution to the program.

Our capacity to listen enables us to connect with others. Without it, we block the possibilities that exist in our relationships. When we learn to master the three distinctions of listening—listening for clarity, listening for understanding, and listening for partnership—we can add a great deal to the quality of our connection with others and provide a structure that supports the context of true partnership.

## AUTHENTIC SPEAKING: EXPRESSING YOUR PERSPECTIVE

The other side of the coin is speaking authentically. To speak authentically is to be open, honest, direct, straight, natural, and genuine in our communications. It means to speak the truth for you—the world from your point of view and perspective. The fundamental goal behind authentic speaking is not to impress, persuade, be liked by, convert, or invalidate another. It is to express what you see and explain why you see that way. By doing so, others have a better idea of who you are and to whom they are relating.

Most of us don't talk straight. Our communication comes from a drive to look good or be appropriate rather than to say what we actually want to say. We speak more of what we think the other person wants to hear instead of our honest perception of the situation. For example, examine any major impediment to customer satisfaction in an organization and trace the communication flow required to resolve it. You will find a communication process that is more grounded in being liked and being nice to one another than in satisfying the organization's so-called commitment to the customer.

Here is what I mean. In training courses I do an activity called the "unspoken communication exercise." It is adapted from an exercise developed by Chris Argyris of Harvard (Argyris 1990, 16). In this process, participants are asked to identify a problem they are having that inhibits their performance. They then imagine the conversation they would have with the individual responsible for resolving the issue. The participants then identify what they are really thinking but not saying—the unspoken conversation. I then ask the participants to list the reasons they don't speak the unspoken communication. The responses are really interesting. Here are a few of them:

- I don't want to upset the other person.
- I don't want to come off as a troublemaker.
- It won't do any good.
- I'm concerned about some form of retribution or reprisal.
- It's not professional.
- I might be wrong.

Participants are then asked to list the outcomes of not speaking the unspoken communication. The list usually includes these outcomes:

- The problem doesn't go away.
- Frustration and stress increase.
- The relationship lacks trust and respect.
- The problem festers until it blows up later.
- Personal and organizational effectiveness are limited.

The unspoken communication in a relationship is very costly. In fact, most relationships are shaped more by what is *not* said than by what is said. If you examine the reasons we don't express the unspoken communication—why we withhold ourselves—you will discover that they are grounded in the drift. The conventional model of relating to others based on a paradigm of separateness and power and control shapes what we say and what we don't say.

I am surprised at the amount of time we don't speak straight to others at home and at work. As a result, there is a tremendous impact on our relationships and a huge drain on our productivity. The amount of time we spend beating around the bush and not dealing directly with each other is astonishing and saddening. What a waste of the human potential that exists in our organizations, and what a waste of the love and regard for our family and friends.

We carry tremendous burdens when we withhold our thoughts, feelings, and beliefs, when we try to say what we think the other person wants to hear, or when we simply cover up what we've said and done. This absolutely limits our ability to build true partnership. A relationship based on true partnership demands and then allows us the freedom for total self-expression. It is a relationship where we are safe to be ourselves, and therefore we are safe to learn, grow, and develop.

True partnership calls for us to raise the bar in straight talk and authentic communication. For many of us there is a risk in speaking straight, yet this risk is only an illusion we carry to the future from our past interactions—interactions inside the drift. When you come from power and control and right–wrong, there is a risk in speaking straight. You will find, however, that is not the case in coming from true partnership. "We would rather be sure of a correctly predicted negative outcome than face the realistic uncertainty of an unpredictable future even if it includes the possibility of great joy and success" (Blanton 1995, 65).

To speak powerfully and authentically in ways that contribute to the relationship involves four elements: speaking from the "I," speaking the truth, speaking from true partnership, and keeping your word.

## Speaking from the "I"

The simplest tool to improve our connection to others is to take responsibility for our own feelings, thoughts, and beliefs by using "I" language. This means using statements that begin with I think, I feel, I believe, I suggest, I need, I would like, I request, or I promise. They are clear, direct, and straightforward communication from our perspective. Using "I" is generally more effective than the alternatives of "you" and "we."

You-messages, such as you should, you are, and you'd better do this, are more aggressive in tone and often create negative reactions. You-messages tend to come across as put-downs, judgments, commands, threats, or labels and generally create hurt feelings, defensiveness, and resistance. This type of communication damages rather than enhances the connections between us.

We-messages are typically more passive in nature. When you or I hide out behind the passive "we," we communicate our thoughts, feelings, and beliefs without having to take responsibility for our communication. Obviously I am not talking about a situation where "we" is accurate, for example, when a team of people is working together. Then it is appropriate to say "We think this would be the best course of action." Just be careful to not use "we" instead of "I" when the message is about *your* point of view.

Here are some examples of the difference between you-messages, passive we-messages, and I-messages:

YOU-MESSAGE: You should get out of the drift and utilize the true partnership model.

PASSIVE WE-MESSAGE: We think that true partnership is the best way to relate to others.

I-MESSAGE: I think true partnership is a very powerful way to relate to other people.


YOU-MESSAGE: You need to get this taken care of.

PASSIVE WE-MESSAGE: We have a problem here.

I-MESSAGE: I am upset that this situation has not been cleared up.

This is a very simple concept, but it is more difficult to put into action than most people think. "When you do not express yourself you are undervaluing your own feelings and interests" (Stone, Patton, and Heen 1999, 94).

## Speaking the Truth

One of the most powerful ways to move beyond the hold of the drift and to create a strong connection with others is to tell the truth. The drift shapes what we say and don't say and conditions us to withhold information (as you saw in the unspoken communication exercise). In true partnership we realize the value of the connection and the importance of speaking the truth for that connection.

In his book *Radical Honesty* (1995), Brad Blanton introduces the "Levels of Telling the Truth—Level I: Revealing the Facts, Level II: Honesty about Current Thoughts and Feelings, and Level III: Exposing the Fiction" (65). Following is a brief explanation of each of these levels of truth telling.

*Level I: Revealing the Facts.* This means to constantly tell the truth about the facts of what happened and to clear up the lies from our past or the information we have withheld. If you forgot to process the customer's order on time, tell the truth rather than blaming the shipping department. If you lied about having a college degree on your résumé, go to your boss and get it cleared up. If you told your son you missed his soccer game because your boss made you take on an extra project when you simply got into your work and forgot the time, get it straightened out.

*Level II: Honesty about Current Thoughts and Feelings.* This means admitting how we feel when we feel it, and speaking our unspoken communication out loud. Not being authentic about your current thoughts and feelings is deceitful and manipulative. It says that you don't trust the other person to handle the communication. If you don't think you can meet the deadline your boss established for a certain project, say so. If you are upset with your spouse for not spending enough time with the kids, tell him or her.

*Level III: Exposing the Fiction.* We all create an identity to survive in this world, a mask, if you will, that is actually what other people relate to. Admitting that who we are is different from who we have been pretending to be enables us to be vulnerable and lets other people get to know our authentic self. For many people, the gap between who we are and what we project to the public is the source of great personal stress because we can't be real with the people around us. If you don't know what to do next, if you are uncertain, or if you are afraid, tell the people around you. Withholding information or not telling the truth damages a relationship and is very costly to individual and organizational effectiveness. It prevents people from operating in a true partnership context.

Many people say to me that they could only speak the truth to this extent in a great relationship where they feel very close to the other person. I respond to them with a "which came first, the chicken or the egg" type of question. I ask, "Well isn't it possible that this level of honesty is what creates great relationships?" In other words, maybe it is this kind of authentic communication that generates close relationships instead of the other way around.

Most of the time when we examine "speaking the truth" in our workshops, people discuss the truth with a negative connotation. In other words, they are afraid that what they have to say will have a negative impact on the other person. But I find that we withhold and do not speak positive emotions as well. It seems to me that few people express appreciation and acknowledgment on a frequent basis. As a result, most of us do not feel appreciated for what we provide the people around us, at work and at home.

This shows up loud and clear in our workshops during an appreciation exercise. In this process one person at a time is selected, and

others are asked to deliver a message using I-statements expressing appreciation for what that person has contributed to the
individual or to the team. From the nervous laughs and the embarrassed glances, it is easy to see that communicating in this way is
uncomfortable for most people. It demonstrates how we do not do
it enough. You cannot have a highly effective relationship, a true
partnership, without expressing your appreciation for your partner
to your partner.

Speaking the truth is a critical element of true partnership.
Without it, people are left in doubt about who you are and what
you do, and the quality of the relationship suffers.

## Speaking from True Partnership

Take responsibility for the delivery of your communication to
other people. Although we cannot control other people's reactions,
in true partnership we are responsible for delivering the message
in an effective manner. The best way to do this is to create a framework of partnership before delivering the communication—
especially if you think the message might be construed as "bad
news." Simply put, tell your partner why you want to have a
conversation, what it is about, and why it is important to you. The
key is to approach the situation with a focus on the relationship,
not the individuals. In other words, share both perspectives and
invite the other person to explore the issue with you. Here are
some examples:

"Hey Jennifer, you said something about the new compensation
package yesterday that has bothered me ever since. I know you
have some concerns about how fair it is, and I am worried about the
effect your comments may have on the new people. Can we sit
down and talk about it?"

"Hey boss. Have you got a couple of minutes? I'm still upset
about this morning's planning session. I know you are under the
gun to complete the project by the first of the month, but I have

some real issues about the shortcuts we're taking. I'd like to kick around some thoughts with you."

"Sweetheart, I think you're still mad at me about my trip next week. I know you question the need for the trip when it means I will miss Bobby's birthday, but I feel some pressure to make this customer happy. I want us to talk about it."

When we take the time to establish a framework of partnership for the communication, we have

- set the stage for a more effective conversation.
- let the other person know what the conversation is about so the person isn't surprised.
- gained agreement as to whether the time is right and the subject matter works for the other person so he or she will be more engaged in the conversation.
- respected the rights of the other person instead of just dropping our needs on that person when it works for us.
- eliminated much of the source of defensiveness by presenting both viewpoints and inviting the other person to explore the issue with us.

It is important to remember that it's not so much what we say—what is important is the context we have created that establishes the meaning of what we say.

## Keeping Your Word

Doing what you say you are going to do adds a great deal to authentic communication. By keeping our word we establish credibility for what we say, and we become more powerful speakers. When we don't do what we say we are going to do, people don't listen to us with the same confidence, and it invalidates future communication. In addition, we create a break in trust—perhaps the most essential element of working and living together.

For the most part, we just don't do what we say we are going to do. I have had clients and prospective clients say things like these. "I'll call you back by the end of the day"—and I don't ever hear from them. "Send me the proposal by overnight mail, I'll review it with my boss and get back to you by Friday"—and they don't call nor do they return any phone calls. "I'll call you at 1:30 tomorrow"—and again no call, no return of my calls, no communication ever again! What a sad commentary on business life today. One of these examples was even from a guy who wanted his team to go through the training course on partnership because "they never do what they say they are going to do!" Another one of the examples is from someone who said to me, "I don't understand why my people don't take me seriously." From my conversation with others, these are not rare occurrences.

Our word is all we have of true value. It damages relationships with others and our relationship with ourselves when we carry the burden of not being true to our word. I do not mean this to be an esoteric comment on morality or people's integrity. I forward this communication as a contribution because it is essential to what we are examining—the quality of our relationships with others. It is quite simply this: When you and I do not do what we say we are going to do, or we do not tell the truth, or we withhold information, it inhibits our ability to generate true partnership with others and that limits our joy, satisfaction, and accomplishment in life.

When we communicate from true partnership, we talk straight and follow up on our promises and commitments; we honor and keep our word. This is what strengthens our connection to others. It's like the partnership between two trapeze artists. When one lets go of the swing, does two flips and reaches out to be caught, the other person had better be there. Inside of true partnership, people will be there—no questions asked. So consider that true partnership is where your partner can let go of the swing knowing that you will be where you said you were going to be or do what you said you were going to do.

## COMMUNICATING IN ACTION

Here is an example of the principle of communicating in action. I once worked with a woman who had her own veterinary practice. We'll call her Louise. The practice included Louise, her partner, a receptionist, and two technicians. When she came to me, Louise was very upset with the receptionist, Martha, and wanted some help in dealing with the situation. It seems that Martha was creating a lot of problems within the team and had been abrupt with a couple of customers. Louise had tried talking to her in many different ways, but she was worried because she didn't want to upset Martha and have her walk out, as Louise needed her right now. Through our conversations, Louise noticed several things:

- She was immersed in the drift; she saw Martha as the enemy who needed to be fixed.
- She had a lot of judgments about Martha regarding the way she dressed and the way she talked to people.
- She had not really listened to Martha.
- She was using subtle forms of power and control as the boss to try to get Martha to change.
- She had a whole lot of unspoken communication that she was holding back, which left her even more resentful toward Martha.
- She was resigned about ever making a difference with Martha and was ready to fire her.

Once Louise saw that this approach wasn't doing any good, she decided to try something different. During one of our coaching sessions focusing on the principles of true partnership, Louise developed and implemented these steps over the next several weeks:

- She created the context that Martha was her partner and that they were climbing a mountain roped together. In other words, they had an interdependent relationship where they would succeed or fail together.

- She then decided to speak all of the unspoken communication that she had been withholding. After all, she had nothing to lose.
- She sat down and framed the conversation with Martha, saying that she was committed to having a partnership with her and wanted to work things out between them.
- She delivered the unspoken communication by using I-statements without blaming Martha or making her wrong.
- She listened to Martha and understood her point of view, thus diffusing Martha's emotions.
- She also asked Martha for her opinion on what was going on and specifically her viewpoint about Louise's management and leadership style.

The final result was that most of the problems between them were resolved and through the conversation Louise discovered that Martha had some physical problems that left her tense and anxious. Martha decided to leave as she wasn't that happy in the job, but she didn't leave in a rush or a huff. Instead, they worked out a transition plan that benefited both of them and left no unresolved resentment in the relationship.

So instead of climbing the mountain roped to someone who did not want to be there, Louise was able to safely change partners and continue the ascent with someone committed to the same things.

The principle of communication enables us to move beyond the typical power struggle inherent in trying to get other people to change and to focus instead on what we actually have control over—the quality of our communication. When we do this,

- we gain a clearer understanding of the other person's perspective, and that person feels respected and regarded.
- we communicate our perspective more authentically, and the other person becomes more aware of our point of view.
- we eliminate the defensiveness and resistance that occurs in so many relationships.
- we are able to discover new solutions to everyday problems.

When organizations focus on communication rather than on power and control,

- people become more empowered with less resentment or resignation.
- they create an atmosphere of straight talk and trust.
- policies and procedures are followed with greater commitment.
- less time is wasted on game playing and politics.
- turnover, lawsuits, employee theft and sabotage, strikes, and work slowdowns are reduced.

It doesn't do any good to waste our time, energy, and resources trying to get other people to do what we want them to do. You and I cannot mold someone else's thinking or behavior. Give it up! Quit judging and blaming others. Look instead at what's missing in the quality of the connection—the communication. Where can you listen more empathically? Where can you speak authentically? These are the things that really count and that open the door to the possibility that inside of the relationship we can create something that will work for the relationship.

# 5 EXPANDING: MOVING BEYOND EITHER–OR THINKING

*If we want to coexist with another person, we must see that his or her certainty—however undesirable it is to us—is as legitimate and valid as our own.* —Fritjof Capra

---

In true partnership we move beyond the polarizing effects of either–or and right–wrong and look for an expanded context that includes and honors differing and perhaps even conflicting points of view. It is not enough to simply tolerate diverse viewpoints. True partnership represents the acceptance of different viewpoints. This does not necessarily mean the merging of viewpoints into a common voice or diluting viewpoints to arrive at agreement. It does mean that all viewpoints have a right to be heard and that in true partnership one point of view does not reign supreme over another. There are, in fact, many truths in any given situation.

---

THE TRADITIONAL PARADIGM OF NEWTONIAN SCIENCE is based on either–or thinking. A fundamental premise of this paradigm is that matter is made up of either a particle or a wave pattern. It can't be both, and the particle is either here right now or it isn't. Newtonian thinking is linear in nature. "In Newtonian physics, there is only one reality at a time . . . a statement is either true or false, a course of action is either good or bad. There can be only one truth, only one best course of action" (Zohar and Marshall 1994, 27).

Quantum thinking, conversely, is nonlinear. It is grounded in a "both–and" approach. In quantum physics, we have an expanded view of matter. Matter has both particlelike and wavelike characteristics, and it can show up as either, depending on what is being measured—what you are looking for. It reminds us that there is always more than one perspective to be considered.

True partnership is not grounded in the typical either–or thinking we find in the drift, that "There is a right way to do this and a wrong way." Instead, in true partnership we come from both–and, asking ourselves, *"What am I willing to learn in this situation?"* In true partnership we recognize the value of diverse viewpoints. We can then use this expanded thinking to choose a more effective course of action.

The principle of expanding (both–and) means that there are many truths in any given situation and that all must be honored before we are able to move beyond the typical stalemate of the right–wrong orientation. This is the premise that enables us to be passionate and committed advocates of our viewpoint and, at the same time, to realize that our way is not the only way to look at things. We can then communicate powerfully and not create the resistance that occurs when we make others wrong. When others know what we stand for and we know what they stand for, we can build real power in true partnership.

A good metaphor for this principle is the story of the blind men examining an elephant. To my recollection, one blind man is feeling the elephant's tail and says, "An elephant is like a rope." The next blind man puts his arms around one of the legs and says, "An elephant is like a tree." And still another says, "No, an elephant is like a snake" after feeling the elephant's trunk. I forget what the others said, but you get the idea. So who was right and who was wrong? They all were depending on their point of view. The world is made up of diverse points of view. There is no right viewpoint.

Diversity issues have been a growing concern for the past decade or two. For the most part when people talk about diversity they are referring to cultural diversity. I think it is much broader than that. In my mind diversity entails not only our cultural backgrounds but also our gender, financial, religious, educational, and political backgrounds and experiences. Diversity includes the differences in our voices, beliefs, points of view, habits of thinking, ways of approaching problems, and philosophies of life. Diversity is everywhere, and we need to realize it.

To say we must tolerate or politely accommodate diversity is insufficient. We must learn to accept and even embrace the diverse nature of our world. The principle of expanding is to say, "Okay, so we are different, and now what do we do?" We do not rank those differences as superior or inferior, right or wrong, instead we look for ways to link our differences and create more powerful relationships.

It is easy to say that another's certainty—what he or she considers to be the truth—is as legitimate and valid as our own, but it is not always easy to put this into practice. From my experience, people often think this is a cute notion, but not a very practical one. But this may just be the crux of true partnership. How do we accept another's viewpoint, one that contradicts our own, as legitimate and valid and build on the differences? This is not an easy question to answer, yet we must each examine it for ourselves.

Here is a simple but powerful story illustrating the challenge we face. A friend of mine once gave me a unique children's book, *The True Story of the 3 Little Pigs!*, by A. Wolf (Scieszka 1989). As the title suggests, it retells the familiar children's story from the point of view of the wolf. The story begins with the wolf, even though he has a bad cold and is not feeling well, baking a cake for his dear grandmother. He runs out of sugar and goes next door to his neighbor, the pig, to borrow a cup of sugar to finish the cake. When the wolf sneezes because of his cold, the house falls down on the pig. The wolf says, "Can you believe it? Who in his right mind would build a house out of straw?" The facts of the story remain the same, but the wolf's interpretation of events is quite different from the classic tale.

It is difficult to hear even a children's story—fiction to begin with—from a different perspective. When I ask people in my workshops to read this story and share their thoughts, I hear some amazing things: "Well, obviously this is not the truth," or "What a cute little story, but it's just a story," or "Why would anyone want to write this story from the bad wolf's viewpoint?" Generally, people believe the pigs' viewpoint states the truth, and we are conditioned to believe that wolves are bad—all from a children's story. We have heard the pigs' version of this story all of our lives and believe it to be the truth. Anything that contradicts this truth is not the truth. Rarely is anyone even willing to accept the possibility that the wolf's version may be the truth.

A simple example, but powerful learning! We think that what we have been told growing up is the truth, and anything else is wrong. When we encounter different beliefs—different truths— we discount them and find ways for our truth to be right.

## MOVING BEYOND RIGHT–WRONG
## COMMUNICATION TO DIALOGUE

People from different backgrounds have different assumptions and opinions, different points of view, and therefore, different truths. Most people feel the need to protect and defend their assumptions and opinions as the truth—setting up a right–wrong orientation. I recall a recent conversation in a training program wherein a senior salesperson was blasting an attorney from the company's legal department. It seems that the attorney was asking the salesperson to clarify some information before she would approve the client contract he had submitted. The salesperson spent a great deal of time defending his viewpoint. He was more experienced than the attorney was, he knew the client better than she did, and as he said to the group, "Since when did the home office interfere with salespeople trying to bring in new business?" He was, in effect, enrolling the rest of the group in his point of view. At the next break I overheard him still talking to a small group of people about the issue. Often we feel that our opinions are so true that we cannot avoid trying to convince, persuade, or pressure other people to see how wrong they are to disagree with us.

Relationships thus become a struggle of opinions, and the one who is the most determined to win *will* win. This is why many conversations take on the flavor of a debate. Listen to any conversation at home or at work; most of the time you will hear this right–wrong debate going on. In a recent session with an organization's executive team, someone very innocently said, "I'm not sure if this merger really helps us that much." Suddenly someone else jumped in and said, "Growth is the only way we will be able to survive in the current marketplace." This prompted the first individual to defend his position with more facts and data and concerns over the present situation in the company. And then the second person responded with more facts, data, and opinions. Then everyone else took sides. It took over an hour to end the debate. While it is true the issue needed to be raised for group discussion, the right–wrong debate did nothing to contribute to making an effective decision.

In another example brought up in class, one participant acknowledged that the previous evening he and his wife had gotten into a disagreement about a trivial little event. During a conversation later in the evening, they realized that the real upset was not over the particular issue but over who was right and who was not.

Right–wrong conversations generally end up in stalemates. Some have a winner and a loser, with subsequent resentments and hurt feelings. At best these conversations end in a compromise. I think "compromise" is an overrated term. It is usually a cop-out. Usually, a compromise is the best you can achieve in the drift. It's really half I win and half I lose and half you win and half you lose. A compromise may get people past the point of being stuck, but it typically does nothing to resolve the real issues or to strengthen the relationship.

In contrast to typical discussion and debate, dialogue offers an opportunity to move beyond the struggles of right–wrong. Dialogue is a powerful communication tool described by quantum physicist and philosopher David Bohm (1990, 2) this way: "Something more of a common participation, in which we are not playing a game *against* each other, but *with* each other." In a dialogue, participants suspend their assumptions and beliefs and step out beyond what they know to be true. Rather than a conversation where opinions are debated in a right–wrong atmosphere, participants let go of what they already know and explore new territory. "Dialogue encourages an opening up about problems, issues or topics. Because it expands what is being communicated by opening up many different perspectives, we call it a divergent conversation. This is in contrast to discussion or debate that is about narrowing down the conversation to one end result. It is trying to come to closure so that everyone knows what to do. Because of this narrowing down, we call this convergent conversation" (Ellinor and Gerard 1998, 22).

Begin noticing any conversation at home or at work and you will see the difference. In typical conversations we experience the same old patterns of competition, the need to be right, and the usual power plays and gamesmanship. Dialogue, in contrast, offers the opportunity to create possibility—something beyond the drift.

Dialogue is not about trying to change anyone's opinions but is about understanding that people's opinions, their truths, can actually be a contribution to a collective truth. This is perhaps the fundamental purpose of dialogue—to create a shared understanding beyond our individual points of view. After all, collective thought is more powerful than individual thought. Or, as we sometimes say, "True partnership thinking is more intelligent than individual thinking."

The following comparison of dialogue in the context of true partnership and the typical debate from the drift provides a good summary of the differences. This comparison is from a paper prepared by Shelley Berman, based on discussions of the Dialogue Group of the Boston Chapter of Educators for Social Responsibility, and included in the book *Dialogue—Turning Controversy into Community* (Poliner and Benson 1997, 16).

| **DEBATE** | **DIALOGUE** |
|---|---|
| Debate is oppositional; two sides oppose each other and attempt to prove each other wrong. | Dialogue is collaborative; two or more sides work together toward common understanding. |
| In debate, winning is the goal. | In dialogue, finding common ground is the goal. |
| In debate, one listens to the other side in order to find flaws and to counter its arguments. | In dialogue, one listens to the other side(s) in order to understand, find meaning, and find agreement. |
| Debate affirms a participant's own point of view. | Dialogue enlarges and possibly changes a participant's point of view. |
| Debate defends assumptions as the truth. | Dialogue reveals assumptions for reevaluation. |
| Debate causes critique of the other position. | Dialogue causes introspection on one's own position. |
| Debate defends one's own positions as the best solution and excludes other solutions. | Dialogue opens the possibility of reaching a better solution than any of the original solutions. |
| Debate creates a close-minded attitude, a determination to be right. | Dialogue creates an open-minded attitude, openness to being wrong, and an openness to change. |
| In debate, one submits one's best thinking and defends it against challenge to show that it is right. | In dialogue, one submits one's best thinking, knowing that other people's reflections will help improve it rather than destroy it. |
| In debate, one searches for glaring differences. | In dialogue, one searches for basic agreements. |
| In debate, one searches for flaws and weaknesses in the other positions. | In dialogue, one searches for strengths in the other positions. |
| Debate involves countering the other position without focusing on the feelings or relationship and often belittles the other person. | Dialogue involves a real concern for the other person and seeks not to alienate or offend. |

| **DEBATE** *(continued)* | **DIALOGUE** *(continued)* |
|---|---|
| Debate assumes that there is a right answer and that someone has it. | Dialogue assumes that many people have pieces of the answer and that together they can put them into a workable solution. |
| Debate implies a conclusion. | Dialogue remains open-ended. |

Most of the initial work on dialogue focused on meetings and other group sessions, but you can surmise from this list of characteristics that it applies to one-on-one conversations as well. When we effectively listen to the other person, authentically communicate our point of view, move beyond right–wrong and expand our thinking, we create more productive conversations. Through dialogue, the whole structure of right–wrong and defending and protecting opinions will collapse, and we will instead discover sharing, participation, and true partnership.

## MOVING BEYOND EITHER–OR IN OTHER INTERACTIONS

### Results or Relationship

Another area where either–or thinking shows up and limits our options is in the "results or relationship" conversation. Many people feel it is one or the other. Either we focus our efforts on getting results at the cost of the relationship, or we focus on the relationship at the cost of results. This shows up at home and at work, but it is most obvious in the workplace. In meeting after meeting and conversation after conversation, I hear this thinking loud and clear. There is a very prevalent belief that if you focus on the quality of the relationship it is a "touchy-feely" approach that is a nice thing to do but probably won't have a positive impact on results.

Just last week, in a conversation with the CEO of a small high-tech firm, I was surprised again at how this particular kind of either–or thinking dominates our actions. After a thirty-minute conversation during which the CEO complained to me about the relationship problems between several of his key staff people, he said, "But really I can't focus on this issue right now. We are under a lot of pressure to hit our numbers this quarter." He just didn't see that resolving the relationship issues would probably have the greatest impact on the results.

It is time to move beyond a "results or relationship" approach and see that results are dependent on relationship. It is important to expand our thinking and create a new approach.

## Nice or Not Nice

In Chapter Four, I explained the unspoken communication exercise in which workshop participants examine what keeps them from speaking the unspoken in an interaction and the consequences of not speaking the unspoken communication. It is all about being nice or not nice. Most people are either nice or not nice. There is nothing in between, and there are no other options. So, given the opportunity to speak our point of view, which might resolve a problem, many of us do not do so because expressing our beliefs might be taken as not nice. The result? The problem persists.

Most of us were brought up to be nice, so typically we don't tell the truth, we withhold information, we suppress our opinions, we say what we think the other person wants to hear, we sugarcoat our message, we beat around the bush, or we walk on eggshells. The bottom line is that we go around being nice to each other and don't accomplish what we're after. Be careful how you interpret this, because I am not saying, "be not nice or mean." This is the perception to get past in order to be more effective.

True partnership offers us a new context that enables us to transcend the limitations of nice and not nice. You can deliver tough messages such as "sell more" or "cut costs" or "do your homework" in a way that does not damage the relationship. True partnership enables us to speak very straightforwardly with people with greater honesty, openness, and authenticity without damaging the relationship.

## Authoritative or Permissive

Another example of either–or that limits our relationships is being authoritative or permissive. The thinking goes that if you are not one then you are the other. In other words, if I do not take charge and take control in an authoritative way, I must swing to the other end of the continuum and do nothing. This is almost epidemic in the ranks of today's middle managers. There has been a great deal written and discussed in the business arena during the past few decades about the ineffectiveness of an authoritative management style. As a result, I find that many managers have become passive to avoid being authoritative. So we find that most managers are either authoritative or permissive, both of which have limitations.

The same is true at home. Most parents are either authoritative or permissive. In our society we see the costs of these two alternatives everywhere. Much of what upsets us in today's society gets traced back to the way we raise our children. Many people, so-called experts included, believe that as parents we have become too permissive, and they advocate more authoritative parenting. But merely swinging back to the other end of the continuum is not the answer. True partnership provides a way to expand our perspective so we are not limited to one end of the continuum or the other.

The either–or mentality of the drift limits us in many ways. Many people listen from an agree–disagree standpoint, noticing only whether they agree or disagree with what is being said rather than listening to what the speaker is saying. In many organizations we constantly hear the debate of short-term or long-term results as if you cannot have both. And at home I hear people talking about the difference between being a parent or a friend, as if the two are incompatible.

## EXPANDING IN ACTION

Todd is the vice-president of a major insurance company that acquired another company with a large call center in St. Louis. Knowing that research shows that more than eighty percent of all mergers and acquisitions fail to produce the expected outcomes due primarily to the failure to merge the organizational cultures—traditional either–or thinking—Todd made the cultural transition a priority. The typical challenges of a merger were compounded in this instance by the fact that the St. Louis call center had been owned by five different companies over the past twenty years, and many of the people working there had been there for those transitions. They were nearly at a point of "Ho-hum, so what else is new?" and paid scant attention to anything Todd and other executives of the new organization said.

Todd kept waiting for these workers to step up to the plate and play the game, and they kept saying "What game?" Meetings and other conversations didn't accomplish much because everyone kept presenting and then protecting their point of view about how things should be done. There was an obvious we–they orientation between the old and the new, and everyone had to pretty much decide which team they were on. Both sides kept making the other wrong. The people who had been there for a while said the new people were moving too fast and there was nothing new from the previous transitions that they had been through. The new people kept making the existing people wrong for not moving fast enough. It was a classic case of right–wrong thinking and clearly demonstrated the limitations of that approach. You can imagine the conversations that went on behind the scenes in the employee cafeteria and elsewhere—and meetings were a nightmare. The polarization of viewpoints was obvious, as it is in most organizations going through similar changes. While everyone was being nice during this getting-to-know-you period, the unspoken communication was deafening. Who was right and who was wrong was in the background of nearly every interaction.

The key point here is that these were all good people. Their hearts were in the right place. No one was consciously out to destroy anyone. There was a lot of talent and experience going to waste simply because they didn't have access to something else. The traditional strategies for enhancing teamwork were not going to provide what was necessary. Only through true partnership could we accomplish what was necessary.

During several sessions with the executive team, the fundamentals of true partnership were introduced and a new context was designed that represented the old and the new. Through the use of both–and thinking, powerful teamwork appeared. Once we developed a new game, people could see how their particular experience and point of view could contribute to the total picture. We had to first examine and then break up the customary either–or thinking and the typical right–wrong approach to problem solving. This new context didn't come out of standard planning sessions. It only emerged after group dialogues and many one-on-one conversations that included getting the underlying assumptions out on the table and listening to all points of view before creating a unifying approach.

And one year later, Todd said, "If we hadn't taken the time to move beyond the either–or mentality in merging the two organizations, there is no telling how much we would be behind where we are now in accomplishing our goals and objectives."

The either–or mentality of the drift is limiting and extremely costly. In each and every one of our relationships we can see the results of either–or thinking. At home, in the workplace from the boardroom to the manufacturing floor, in government from city council meetings to the halls of Congress, and between racial, ethnic, and religious groups we see relationships where people get stuck and positional in protecting their point of view and purposefully or inadvertently make others wrong. The outcomes? Nothing gets resolved, or at least not much.

When we operate from the principle of expanding, we open the door to new perspectives and new approaches to help solve the problems we face. Instead of an either–or focus, we can entertain many different possibilities. Here are some of the advantages to operating from a position of both–and:

- We treat others with greater regard and respect when we honor their point of view.
- We become better listeners.
- We develop more effective solutions to problems when we see more sides to an issue.
- We do not waste time trying to prove we are right.
- We are open to new options when we stop defending our own position.
- We have productive conversations rather than debates when addressing an issue.
- We build a greater sense of integration and participation into the decision-making process.

Organizations also benefit from both–and thinking:

- They are more open to change and can respond more quickly to meet the needs of the marketplace.
- Leadership is more effective, and fewer decisions are made that don't work due to the limited viewpoint of the decision maker.
- Innovative thinking and creativity are encouraged, and the atmosphere is action-oriented rather than stagnant.
- Diversity is celebrated, not just tolerated, and individuals are encouraged to speak from their different viewpoints in a respectful way.

The principle of expanding by operating from both–and means that through true partnership we value diverse viewpoints, learn from them, build on them, and discover totally new approaches that make us more effective as individuals and as groups.

# 6 Observing: What We See Depends on Who We Are

*The ability to perceive or think differently is more important than knowledge gained.* —David Bohm

The way we see the world is known as observing, and most of us think that what we see is fixed. That is, there is a world "out there," and we are merely witness to it. This is inconsistent with the principles of the new sciences. One of the fundamentals of quantum thinking is that reality emerges from our observations. In the quantum world the observer plays an essential role in bringing forth the very situation that he or she is observing. Therefore, the decisions or interpretations we make about our world are shaped by our observations. The decisions we make and the interpretations we apply are made from who we are—through the lens of our personal history. What we see depends on who we are. Once we understand the principle of observing, we no longer need to be dependent on existing perspectives that fail to serve us. We can take responsibility for our view of the world and, if necessary, change the way we observe.

THE WORLD OF NEWTONIAN PHYSICS is a rigid world of fixed identities and predictable patterns. Many refer to it as a mechanistic view. As such, the universe is seen as a big machine with everything in its place doing what it should. This Newtonian model requires the acceptance of black and white thinking, structured rules, and indisputable truths. It is a simple world that thrives on certainty, predictability, and knowing. Using this model, we have been taught to understand observing as a process of witnessing what is out there, independent of us as the observer. In this world we are observers of fact that we validate by saying things like, "That's just the way he/she/it is."

The quantum world is complex, ambiguous, and uncertain. Rather than being fixed and predictable, it is full of possibilities. In the quantum world the observer plays an essential role in bringing forth the very situation that he or she is observing. As an observer, we participate in creating our world.

As I have explained previously, one of the fundamental premises of quantum physics is the wave–particle duality. Matter is composed of both wavelike and particlelike characteristics, and it has the possibility of being either. One of the basic and most famous experiments that formed the foundation of the quantum model is the two-slit experiment. In simple terms, the experiment proved that if instruments were set up to look for and measure particles, what the physicist saw was particles. When the instruments were set up to look for and measure waves, what the physicist saw was waves. In other words, how we observe any given situation evokes one of the underlying options; what we look for is what we see.

The significance of this fundamental concept is radical not only in the world of science but also in our everyday lives. All of a sudden you and I as observers see we have some responsibility in how our world and the people in it appear to us. If this is the case and we don't know it, we are at the mercy of our perceptions, victims to our own observations. If this is the case and we recognize it, we have tremendous power in any situation. We can then ask ourselves, *"What is another way I can view him/her/it?"* We are then no longer a helpless pawn to forces beyond our control, deceived by our observations.

There is another essential point to address here. People tend to react to us in the context we have created. If we expect our mother-in-law to be nosey or our boss to be controlling, we may in fact be setting them up to appear to act that way. "If one approaches another man with a fixed 'theory' about him as an 'enemy' against whom one must defend oneself, he will respond similarly, and thus one's 'theory' will apparently be confirmed by experience" (Bohm 1980, 6).

## REALITY EMERGES FROM OBSERVATION

Why is it that you and I can go to the same party or see the same movie and come home with totally different perceptions? It is because we have different ways of evaluating what we like and what we don't like. In both of these situations most of us are aware that whether or not we had fun at the party or enjoyed the movie is a personal opinion, a personal decision. However, we fail to carry this awareness into other areas of our lives.

Consider that *everything* we experience is an opinion—a personal decision. As observers we always view a particular event, situation, or person from a specific perspective, a specific point of view. Our reality—our experience in life—emerges from our process of observation and the decisions we make about what we see: "We don't see things as they are, we see things as we are" (Maturana and Varela 1992, 242).

The manner in which we observe is shaped by a context. This context shapes how we view the world, and therefore it shapes how things appear to us and the subsequent decisions we make about what we see. Since a context is primarily influenced by our past, we actually view any particular situation through the lens of our personal history. We see what we have been taught to see, what we have been conditioned to see, and what our experience has us expecting to see. The particular lens we look through definitely filters and shapes what we see—and what we don't see. This can be illustrated graphically as the process of observing (see next page).

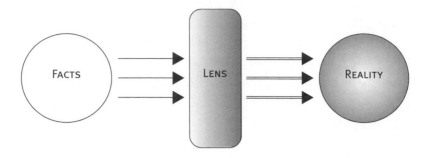

We all look at the facts—what is actually happening—through our personal lens, our filters, and the result is what we call our reality, or our experience. The point to remember is that typically we take it as the truth—that this is what is happening. More accurate words to describe "reality" in the right-hand circle are opinion, perspective, point of view, judgment, interpretation, or illusion. In other words, what we experience is simply our inter-pretation, or our point of view, or our illusion shaped by the con-text we bring to the table. The danger comes from not knowing how the principle of observing works, or forgetting about it.

I like to do a lot of black and white photography and I use filters frequently. They do the same thing to the pictures I take as our perceptual filters do to us—they distort reality. If I take pictures through an orange filter, it causes greater contrast between the fluffy white clouds and the deep blue sky so the final picture looks as if the clouds literally jump out of the sky. I can use a star filter to create a burstlike effect from lights in the picture. Photograph-ing a candle flame with this filter makes it look as if beams of light are shooting out from the flame. Or I can use another filter to soften the lines of the human face and make portraits look much more pleasing. Our filters—the way we perceive the world around us—do much the same thing. They distort reality—what actually exists.

In our classroom training sessions I ask people to look around the room and identify as many *blue* objects as they can. After thirty seconds or so, I ask them to close their eyes and list everything they saw that was *red*. After the chuckles subside, they admit they did not see any red objects. Our process of observing works in this same way. If our experience—and, therefore, our context—says the world is blue, we filter out everything else and all we see is blue. Then we think, or say, "See, the world is blue." Our filters screen out certain things and let others in. They allow us to see only that evidence that matches our beliefs. In this way the manner in which we observe becomes self-fulfilling and self-perpetuating. Therefore, once you and I have a particular context that we operate from, further evidence tends to reaffirm that context and make it *"The right way to be."*

We tend to block out or discount information that does not agree with or fit into the context that shaped our filters to begin with. Scientists call this an anomaly—information that does not agree with or cannot be explained within the existing paradigm. For example, if I have a belief that I cannot hit a good backhand shot in tennis, that would pretty much be my experience. Even if I hit a winning backhand shot down the line and past you for a point, I would probably discount it as a lucky shot or a fluke. Why? Because "I can't hit a backhand," and I must rationalize any shot that invalidates my fundamental belief and way of observing. You and I do the same thing with almost everyone and everything every day.

We have been using visual examples, but our filters operate in much the same way when we listen. What we hear when we listen to others is not necessarily what they are saying, rather it is our interpretation of what they are saying. Let's assume that I am your boss and I come up to you at the end of the month and say, "Nice job on the month-end report. It was very well organized and on time." Also, assume that you don't trust me. Either you don't trust authority figures, or you don't trust guys named Carl who wear glasses. (My name is Carl and I wear glasses.)

It is important to note here that these beliefs (the context you operate from) have nothing to do with me. The beliefs come from your past relationship with authority figures or with guys named

Carl who wear glasses. Perhaps when you were in grade school some guy named Carl who wore glasses stole your lunch. When something like that happens, you and I have a tendency to form a belief such as "you can't trust guys named Carl who wear glasses." Once that is done, further evidence reinforces that belief—even if it is not so. For example, years later in high school you go back to your locker after lunch and find that someone stole the new jacket you got for your birthday. My locker is just down the hall, and your first thought is that "Carl took it." You then take whatever action you think is necessary, convinced that Carl took your jacket. But later in the week you find out that Sam took your jacket. When I ask participants in our class what they would then think, I hear things such as, "Well Sam just beat Carl to it" or "Carl put him up to it!" The point is that I (Carl) don't stand a chance with you until you become aware of the way you observe and decide to alter the way you look at the world. Now, back to my story.

So, I am your boss and I say to you, "Nice job on the month-end report. It was very well organized and on time." I then ask people in my workshop what they would think or hear given that they don't trust me as their boss. I hear responses such as "Yeah, that's the good news, now when is the hammer going to fall?" or "You're just trying to butter me up to get something" or "Wonder what he wants now?" So here I am, paying you a compliment, but it means something entirely different to you.

Our positive beliefs set us up to see the world in a specific way, and that can be just as limiting as so-called negative beliefs. As an example, let me share a personal story. My mother is extremely organized, and growing up in our home personal organization was paramount. In fact, I was taught to believe that being organized is the key to success and accomplishment. It seems to work for me. In my opinion, one of my best characteristics and an essential ingredient of my success is my ability to have a very organized approach to any situation. The context "being organized is a good thing" shapes my life and the way I observe others.

So why would this be limiting? As you have probably heard many times, our weaknesses are simply extensions of our strengths. Many times it may be more effective to simply jump into a situation rather than to take the time to get organized. In addition, organization becomes the basis for my judgments of others. For example, if I were to walk through an office as a new manager, the first thing I would see is how organized people appear to be. From that observation, I would probably decide who is capable and who is not. You know what I mean—those nasty first impressions that are so difficult to overcome. Also, when coaching people, my own context would come into play. If you were to ask me what you could do to be more effective, the first thing I would suggest is to become more organized. And that may or may not be the first thing you need to do.

The bottom line about our filters is that most of us are not very good at seeing or hearing what is actually going on. Our filters distort our thinking and what we see and hear. The real problem is that how we react to others—our behavior in relating to them—is shaped more by our context and the interpretation of what they say or do than by what actually happens.

## WE ARE ALL UNIQUE OBSERVERS

It is important to note that each and every one of us is a different observer. Each of us has a unique way of observing what shapes we see and hear. Our personal lens or filters are shaped by many factors:

- Personal experiences
- Family environment
- Age
- Geographic background
- Economic background

- Religion or religious experience
- Race and ethnic heritage
- Gender

Every one of us has a unique context for our lives and a unique way of observing, so we have different perspectives and different interpretations of the people, places, and events in our lives. But because of our filters, we think our perspective is the right one. This is one of the factors that sets up the right–wrong orientation we examined earlier. It is essential in true partnership that we understand this and recognize that what we see in life is only our point of view, our perspective, our opinion—our interpretation of the facts. It is all something that we make up.

This distinction between observing and the fact that we are all different observers has significant implications. Understanding these implications sets the foundation for profound change.

## CHANGING THE WAY WE OBSERVE

It is important to recognize that the way we observe is not set in cement. We are not limited to forever observe the way we presently do. We can learn and change the way we observe. But we cannot make significant and sustainable changes until we know that filters exist and shape our experience. With that knowledge we can begin to understand what filters we presently have and how they may limit us. Then we can begin to discover other filters that might better serve us.

This is the process that many people refer to as waking up— recognizing that the way we observe may not be the only way and opening ourselves to discovering new ways. Powerful learning comes from reflecting on and examining the way we observe in any given situation. As noted psychologist and philosopher R. D. Laing (1970, 17) said, "The range of what we think and do is limited by what we fail to notice. And because we fail to notice that we fail to notice, there is little we can do to change until we notice how failing to notice shapes our thoughts and deeds."

When we shift the way we observe, it is as if we see new things. People, situations, and events show up differently. When we operate from the drift, we see people as objects that are different from us that we need to control so that we will not be controlled by them. However, when we operate from true partnership, we see the exact same person as an individual with whom we are already connected. If we want to improve that connection, we understand that we need to improve the communication. Again, this is the exact same person. With one set of filters, the drift, we strategize on how to get the upper hand in difficult situations. With the filters of true partnership, we look at how to alter our listening and how to communicate more authentically to accomplish the desired results.

Who or what we regard as a problem and the possibilities we see for change all depend on the type of observer we are. When we shift how we observe, we see new approaches to problems and discover new possibilities.

## OBSERVING IN ACTION

Several years ago I worked on a project with the California Youth Authority. We took fifteen young men between the ages of eighteen and twenty-four who were incarcerated and facilitated the partnership course to provide them with the skills to change their lives when they were paroled. (This is the very same course we provide to corporations.) The group consisted of African Americans, Hispanics, Asians, and Caucasians.

Originally I thought I was there to teach them something, but was I surprised. When I walked into the room for the first of six sessions, I was immediately confronted with my beliefs, judgments, opinions, and interpretations. What I saw was a group of what appeared to me to be derelicts who had committed crimes and should be locked up forever. Gang members with tattoos and appearances that would have intimidated me beyond belief had I seen them on the street at night. And my first reaction was, "What am I doing here?"

And their nonverbals were almost yelling, "What does this ol' white guy think he's going to tell us?" I also noticed that each ethnic group sat together with their chairs arranged so they didn't have to look at the other groups. Talk about a tough audience!

Then miracles began to happen. Using the core principles of true partnership, we had an authentic conversation about the ways we observed each other, the interpretations we made, and how that limited our ability to connect. For the next few hours and during subsequent sessions we spoke honestly, became more willing to fully express ourselves, learned to listen to each other and understand what the other person's world was like, and became responsible for our interpretations of how we see the world.

Once we changed our focus from seeing each other as objects to try and mold as we wanted them to be to seeing each other as human beings with whom we are already connected and related, we profoundly enhanced the quality of the relationships. Improve the quality of the relationship and you fundamentally improve the quality of the results.

At the end of the first session I noticed a shift in how I was seeing these guys, and I looked forward to coming back. By the end of the program there was a significant difference in the quality of the communication and the relationships in the room. Even the members of different ethnic groups merged together and began to build strong bonds. They even expressed their concerns about going back to the prison community that would not support their new friendships. These young men were very clear about how peer pressure from their particular communities would stifle their application of much of what they had learned. They each saw that through true partnership they were able to create something that surpassed anything they had experienced before. I learned that beyond their rough appearances they were young men who wanted something different in their lives and the lives of their families, and they just didn't know how to go about getting it.

I must tell you that my cynicism came up frequently. I wanted to make sure that I was not being "conned" as I was told often happens. I frequently questioned the guard and the Catholic Chaplain who attended all sessions, and they both assured me they had never seen anything like this before. In fact, Father Conner said, "In a short period of time the students seemed to identify the impact their mind-sets had on their lives, which resulted in them being incarcerated."

The principle of observing is an essential component of true partnership. It enables us to shift our context from the limitations of the drift to the possibilities of true partnership. When we relate to our world as an *observer-created* reality, we can benefit in these ways:

- We don't freeze people into predictable patterns of behavior; therefore, we have the opportunity to improve the relationship and build true partnership.
- We take more responsibility for our observations and communicate our point of view by saying things like "it seems to me" or "it appears to me," rather than "it is this way." This allows the relationship to transcend the polarization of right–wrong viewpoints.
- We eliminate any sense of powerlessness in relating to others and take greater responsibility for our relationships, our lives, and the results we produce.
- We are more open and not paralyzed by a reality that we initially saw as fixed and predefined.
- We become more able to adapt to rapid changes and more comfortable stepping out and taking risks because we have some sense of control over our reactions.

When we relate to our world as observer-created, our organizations become

- more flexible, more adaptive to change, and more creative.
- less resigned, complacent, and cynical.
- more optimistic with a stronger sense of team morale and motivation.
- a place where everyone has a stronger sense of belonging and takes on a greater responsibility for organizational results.

Since our experience in life is all invented anyway, why can't we invent something that works for us? When we take responsibility for our role in creating the way people appear to us, we open the door for unprecedented, unpredictable changes in our relationships. And, if the kind of results evident in the California Youth Authority course can show up there, they can show up anywhere.

# 7 True Partnership Is an Individual Choice

*People are always blaming their circumstances for what they are. I don't believe in circumstances. The people who get on in this world are the people who get up and look for the circumstances they want and if they can't find them, make them.* —George Bernard Shaw

---

We do not have to adapt ourselves to fit the circumstances, the box we live in. We need not live as if we are pawns to forces beyond our control. We have abilities far in excess of what we have been taught or dared to believe. True partnership provides us with the opportunity to move beyond the limits we have set for ourselves and the constraints of others and break through to new levels of individual and group effectiveness. There are no saviors to rescue us or deliver us to a new world. The job of transforming ourselves, our families, our organizations, and our world is up to each of us. It is a personal choice that you and I make many times each and every day.

---

THE QUALITY OF OUR RELATIONSHIPS has absolutely nothing to do with the other person. Who the other person is, or what they do or say, has nothing to do with the quality of the relationship we have with them—nothing, none, no impact. Notice that I did not say what they say or do is not important. What I did say is the other person's actions have nothing to do with how you or I go about relating to them.

This may sound like an outrageous statement, and you may be thinking it can't possibly be true. Every piece of evidence that we have seems to contradict this. We can all point to people in our lives with whom we could never build a relationship. You could say that a relationship is between two people and that it takes both people to make it work. Everyone knows that other people say things or do things that damage our relationship with them. We all have many examples of bosses, customers, people in other departments, spouses, children, or friends who are just not willing to do what they need to do to relate to us better. So how can I be claiming that the quality of our relationships has nothing to do with the other person?

I am asking you to consider that you and I are totally responsible for the quality of our relationships—that we have the power to decide whether they work or not and to create extraordinary relationships. We are not limited to trying to get the other person to change, or to rationalizing our way around what they do, or to acquiescing our needs, wants, and desires. We can examine our own assumptions and beliefs. The context we bring to the table, how we are speaking and listening, and how we are dealing with disagreements and conflicts are the things that shape relationships. And these are the things that we have control over.

True partnership is not simply a "nicer" version of the power and control model. It is not some nicey-nice game to play. It is not about the soft skills referred to by people in many companies. It is not about the comfort of the status quo. It is not about waiting for others to take the first step. True partnership will not come to us through osmosis while we sleep or through positive thinking and affirmations.

True partnership will live only when we embrace it and put it into action as individuals. In each and every interaction you and I have, we have a choice. We can stay in the drift and perpetuate the power and control model, or we can stand for true partnership and the possibilities it represents. Most people think they already operate with a choice. In my experience this is rarely the case. What many people see as their choice is the "either this or that" thinking of the drift. In other words, they have very little choice in actuality. One of the people I am coaching right now is Melanie. We started out working on building her real estate business, but the real issue became her relationship with her husband. She felt that either she had to give in to her husband's concerns over the hours she worked or she had to leave the relationship and go on her own. She was actively considering the latter as she saw no other alternatives. Melanie said she had "tried everything else" and she was frustrated and resigned.

To me, that was no choice at all. These were simply two options within the drift. Once we addressed the true partnership context and focused on the quality of the communication, she made real headway in both the relationship with her husband and the success of her business. Melanie saw how the drift limited her communication skills and the results she produced. She realized that things changed only when she became aware of the power of the drift and the importance of the communication. The only true choice we have is to stay stuck with some variation of the drift or to let go of our habitual ways of thinking and acting and explore the new possibilities of true partnership.

A fundamental shift in the way we observe and therefore act in our relationships calls for the courage to take a stand for our life and then to take actions consistent with that stand. It takes courage to break up existing patterns in established relationships or to step out on a limb and behave differently in creating new relationships. It takes courage to be accountable for your life rather than blaming other people or circumstances. "If you want to change the world, you have to start with your own life—you must become the change you want to see in the world" (Handy 1998, 103).

## THE DRIFT AND TRUE PARTNERSHIP: COMPARING THE TWO MODELS

We can now compare the familiar context of being separate and autonomous—the drift—with the new true partnership context. This new context provides a way of looking at the world that offers solutions to issues and problems not apparent in the old model, and it provides an opportunity to build relationships that otherwise might not be possible. While the comparison is displayed in a side-by-side table, remember that this is not an either–or situation. A shift in the way we observe does not invalidate our current or past observation. Like climbing a mountain, the higher we climb, the broader the view, which does not invalidate the view from lower altitudes.

| THE DRIFT | TRUE PARTNERSHIP |
|---|---|
| *Separate and Autonomous* | *Interdependent Parts of the Whole* |
| Focus on the individual | Focus on the relationship |
| "I can do it on my own." | "What can we accomplish together?" |
| Sets up we–they and blame | Establishes "us" and builds accountability |
| *Connected through Power and Control* | *Connected through Communication* |
| Focus on using power and control to get things done | Focus on the communication to get things done |
| Emphasis is on molding others' behavior | Emphasis is on listening and speaking |
| Sets up win–lose | Creates a "win" for the relationship |
| *Operate from Either–Or Thinking* | *Operate from Both–And Thinking* |
| There is one singular truth | There are many truths |
| Relationships become polarized | Relationships become aligned |
| Focus on right–wrong | Focus on "What would work here?" |

| | |
|---|---|
| Conversations become debates | Conversations become dialogues |
| *Relate to the World as Fixed* | *Relate to the World as Observer-Created* |
| People are seen as fixed identities with predictable patterns of behavior | People show up through our observations and interpretations |
| "That's just the way he/she/it is." | "How else can I view him/her/it?" |
| React to circumstances | Responsible for circumstances |
| Live within the box, with fixed boundaries | Live outside of the box, with no boundaries |

## AN INDIVIDUAL CHOICE: TAKING A STAND FOR TRUE PARTNERSHIP

In each and every interaction, we consciously choose which model to use. Do you want to continue relating to others in ways that have been passed down to you by others, or are you willing to cause a revolution in your own thinking and personally experience the value of true partnership? To know whether you are in the drift or creating true partnership, ask yourself these questions:

- Are you looking at the other person as an obstacle to getting what you want, or do you see that person as a partner with whom you could collaborate?
- Are you acting as if it is we–they, or are you looking at this situation from "us"?
- Are you blaming the other person, or are you taking responsibility for the results?
- Is your goal to change the other person, or are you accepting that person and communicating your needs to him or her?
- Are you acting as if your viewpoint is the right one, or are you acting as if the other person's viewpoint is as valid as yours?
- Are you judging, evaluating, or determining whether you agree or disagree with the other person, or are you listening to understand their viewpoint?

- Are you withholding your communication in order to be nice or out of fear of repercussions, or are you speaking in a straightforward manner?
- Do you see the other person or situation as "that's just the way he/she/it is," or are you open to other possibilities?

Ask yourself these questions whenever you feel upset, when you feel blocked or stymied in accomplishing what you want, or if you simply want more out of an already great relationship. Depending on how you answer, you will know very quickly which model you are using and what behaviors will then be appropriate. There is no right or wrong way to be. You just have to look for the most effective course of action.

The shift to a context of true partnership occurs when each of us becomes accountable for our relationships and takes the initiative required to build and maintain productive and satisfying partnerships. To create and sustain a new context requires declaration, commitment, and accountability.

- *Make a declaration of your intentions—the context you wish to create.* You and I need to put our butts on the line by telling others about our commitment to true partnership and what that means for our relationships. Let others know what they can expect from you in your interactions—what they can count on. A public declaration is the first step in creating a new context.
- *Identify the commitments necessary to fulfill your intentions.* Many people feel commitments are too restrictive or involve too much pressure or effort. This is usually because we make commitments for the wrong reasons: So we will look good, because it is the socially acceptable thing to do, or if we commit others will do the same. These are not the most empowering reasons. To bring forth a new context requires that you commit for your own reasons. So the question is, "What do I

need to do and what am I willing to do to move beyond the limitations of the drift and create a new context of true partnership in my life?"

- *Design a system of accountability to fulfill your commitments.* Accountability is another word that is often misused. Many times it is used to beat people over the head when things don't go right. As a result, is it any surprise that many people avoid taking on being accountable? To design a system of accountability, develop a structure that supports you in accomplishing your intentions. I recommend using a coach. Creating a new context is a challenge for many of us because we are accustomed to seeing things in a certain way, making it difficult to see differently. An effective coach can support you in seeing differently. With or without a coach, it is important to realize that you will not always operate from true partnership in relating to others. When those situations occur, forgive yourself (and others) and do not blame or make anyone wrong. Instead, look at what is missing and find behavior that would now put you back on a path that is consistent with your intentions.

President Kennedy went through these steps in 1961 when he created the new context, "put a man on the moon and return him safely to earth by the end of the decade." He made the declaration before Congress, identified the commitments and personally made sure the fundamental commitment of funding was present, and he made NASA accountable for the results. You and I need to take the same steps to experience the real value of true partnership.

## TEN PRACTICES FOR TRUE PARTNERSHIP

A "practice" is an activity that you do repeatedly to become proficient in a specific skill or to bring about a desired result. I have condensed the key ingredients of true partnership and provided practices to help you implement true partnership in each and every one of your interactions.

## Recognize that True Partnership Must Be Generated

True partnership is not our natural way of relating. For most of us it is counterintuitive to the way we have been thinking and acting. It requires that we be accountable for the quality of our relationships, take the initiative in our actions, and move beyond the instinctive and inherited thinking of the drift. We cannot wait for others. We must take the lead to create true partnerships with those around us.

## Understand the Power of Context

Context is the particular frame of reference that shapes the way we perceive the world. It is our mind-set. Context shapes our behavior, the results we produce, and what we judge to be possible or not. It shapes how we perceive others, how we listen, what we say or don't say, and how we approach disagreements and conflicts. The context shapes what we view as a problem, how we go about resolving the problem, and what we consider to be an effective resolution to the problem. Only by altering the underlying context can we fundamentally change the relationships in our lives and, therefore, what we accomplish.

## Expose the Drift

The drift is the instinctive and inherited context that shapes our relationships. The drift limits our possibilities by conditioning us to act in certain ways. Only by exposing these patterns for what they are can we move beyond their grip. In the drift, we see the differences in people and unconsciously rank them as superior or inferior. We separate people into categories of we–they, and when something goes awry, we typically blame others. When operating in the drift, we strategize ways to get other people to do what we want them to do—as if we actually have the power to change their behavior. We come from a right–wrong orientation. And we view others as fixed identities based on our assumptions and beliefs, fitting them into the box of "That's just the way he or she is." Any of these actions are red flags that we are operating in the drift.

## Focus on the Relationship

Rather than focusing on the differences between people and ranking individuals as superior or inferior, see the value of linking. Move past the prejudices, biases, and judgments you bring to the table and concentrate on the quality of the connection. Think in an interdependent fashion. Shift from an "I can do it on my own" mentality to "What can we accomplish together?" Move past the blame of the we–they orientation to "us," and be accountable for the condition of the relationship—the connection.

## Quit Trying to Change People

The quality of the connection is determined by the communication. When things don't happen as you want them to, do not look at what you can do to get the other person to change. Look instead at "What is missing in the communication?" How can you shift the way you are listening or what you are saying or not saying to have an impact?

## Listen Empathically

Quit listening to find out if you agree or disagree with the other person. Listen to understand others' points of view. Remember that their perspective is the truth for them. Do not invalidate their truth by interrupting, judging, or evaluating. Use the skill of active listening to let the other person know that you have thoroughly heard and understood them.

## Speak Authentically

Speak the truth for yourself, realizing that it may not be *the* truth. Be open and honest in your communication. Do not withhold information. Communicate with I-language and take responsibility for your thoughts, feelings, and beliefs. Perhaps the biggest obstacle to a productive, satisfying, and rewarding relationship is what is not said. Learn to notice what is typically unspoken and communicate it responsibly.

## Communicate from Both–And

Do not assume "my way is the right way." Remember that there are many truths in any given situation and that the other person's point of view is as legitimate and valid for him or her as your viewpoint is for you. Practice the dialogue process and learn to have a conversation that surpasses the polarization or stalemate of debate.

## Move Beyond Being Right

Everything you experience in your life is an interpretation. Your perspectives, your points of view, and your opinions are all derived by observing what is actually happening through your filters. Take responsibility that your viewpoint is based merely on who you are and how you are observing. Use "it seems to me" or "from my viewpoint" rather than "it is." For example, say "It seems to me that we are wasting too much time reviewing this proposal" rather than "It is a waste of time to review this proposal."

## Take a Stand

You have a choice. It is your decision to relate to others from the habitual practices of the drift or to generate true partnership. To take a stand is to commit yourself to act consistently with declarations about who you are. To stand for true partnership is to commit yourself to the principles and practices necessary to relate to others from a context of true partnership—not just in those relationships where you think you need to but in all relationships. Be a model of the change you want to see in the world.

## FREQUENTLY ASKED QUESTIONS

To help you integrate the true partnership perspective into your life on a daily basis, I will address four questions that frequently arise for people after they have been exposed to this model.

- How do I utilize the true partnership model when the other person is into power and control?
- When should I give up trying to build a partnership?
- How do I get others to try a true partnership perspective?
- What is the role of a leader in building an organization's culture of true partnership?

The answers to these questions will not only provide a great review of the principles and practices of true partnership but will also give you an opportunity to see ways to weave true partnership into your daily life.

*How do I utilize the true partnership model when the other person is into power and control?*
To begin with, all of us come from power and control. That is the nature of the drift. Realize that whatever the other person is doing or saying is the best he or she can do from the drift. They have the

capacity for true partnership: like you and me, they just need help gaining access to it.

True partnership does not mean building true partnership only with those people committed to true partnership. Rather, this is a perspective that you as an individual create for interacting with others. In my experience, very few people come from a true partnership perspective. Even after reading this book, some people will smile and feel good because it is consistent with the way they think we "should" relate to one another. Oftentimes these people are not aware of the power of the drift in shaping the way they think and act. There seems to be a tremendous disparity for many people between what they say they are committed to and what they actually do. We need to find a way to neutralize the power of the drift so that our habitual ways of relating to people by arguing with them or making them wrong can be changed.

Remember, your belief that "they are into power and control" is simply one interpretation of what is actually going on—it is not *the truth*. You think—actually you make it up—that they are trying to control or dominate you. You are setting it up that they are coming from power and control. To check your perceptions, ask yourself these questions:

- Are you looking at the other person as an obstacle?
- Are you coming from we–they?
- Are you blaming the other person?
- Is your goal to change the other person?
- Are you acting as if your viewpoint is the right one?
- Are you judging and evaluating the other person?
- Are you withholding communication?
- Do you see the other person as "That's just the way he/she is"?

Your honest answers to these questions will help you determine what your goal is in a particular situation. Many times the problem goes away when you change your perspective.

A more pertinent question to ask yourself is: "Am I willing to relate to the other person from true partnership without any change in their behavior?" Literally, if you change your filters—the way you observe the other person—he or she will appear differently. It is all an interpretation; why not decide to make it an interpretation that contributes to your relationship with them?

If your goal is to develop the relationship and transform the outcomes, then you will have a better chance if you take the following action steps:

1. Change your focus from an interpretation that the other person is coming from power and control to one where he or she is your committed partner and needs something in the relationship. The easiest way to do this is to change from focusing on what's wrong to what's right about the relationship.

2. Tell the other person what you are committed to and request that you have a specific conversation about the relationship. For example, "Boss, I'm committed to getting this project done on time but the communication between us seems to be slowing it down. Can we sit down today and talk about it?" Or "Mary (your roommate), I'm committed to having our apartment be a comfortable home for both of us, and I have a sense there is some tension in the air. Can we talk about it?" When I give these examples some people say, "That's not me" or "That's too weird." Saying something like this may seem different because you are not used to coming from true partnership. When you first do anything, a lot of actions seem strange.

3. Listen to the other person. Listen, listen, listen, listen, listen, listen, listen, and then listen some more. There is a good possibility that the other person has never felt heard and understood by you. It does not matter how much you feel that you understand the other person, only when you have used the active listening tool and the other person knows that you

understand him or her will the listening process be complete. As we examined earlier, there is unspoken communication in nearly every conversation. Only when you access what the other person has not been saying will you get the real issue out on the table. Sometimes just getting it out on the table is the only thing necessary to get it resolved.

4. Be authentic and speak the truth for you. Use I-language and the word "seems" for "is." In other words, say "It seems to me . . ." rather than "It is this way . . ." Speak your unspoken communication completely and get it out on the table. This is the only way to get to the crux of the issue and get it resolved. If you don't speak the truth for you, then recognize that the other person is not coming from power and control—you are. You are allowing yourself to be dominated.

5. Explore other options. Do not be limited by what you think is right or what others think is right. Move beyond your point of view and the other person's point of view and explore totally new viewpoints through dialogue.

*When should I give up trying to build a partnership?*

Give up anytime you want. But don't confuse partnership with true partnership. Partnership is a form of relationship primarily established when two or more people are working toward a common goal, but it is cosmetic in nature. True partnership is a context you come from that shapes your actions with others no matter who they are or what they do or whether or not you are working toward the same goal.

You may not always achieve the result you want. True partnership is not a tool to get what you want to have happen. There is no guarantee. Not every problem can be handled through communication, and the fact is that some people are simply not willing to relate to others in this way. It may be too scary or too risky for them, or perhaps they are not capable of moving beyond some deeply held resentment for you or a particular situation. It is important to remember that you are still responsible for your observations—your filters—and the subsequent interpretations. How you react to the person is still only up to you.

I once led a course on true partnership for a group of managers in a large Chicago-based company. The program went very well except for one person who never seemed to get on board with the rest of the group. It just seemed that no matter what I did I was unable to alter the connection with her. At lunch the next day with the group's manager I discovered the underlying issue: this woman was going through a tough divorce and her husband's name was Carl. She was in a space that seemed to prevent us from creating a workable partnership. That does not mean I was not coming from true partnership in relating to her, however.

We all have a picture of a great relationship, but this picture is not the same for everyone. I was once in a romantic relationship with a woman named Rose. We eventually decided that we were not out for the same things in our lives, but we still came from true partnership in ending the relationship in the form that it had existed. In other words, although our "partnership" ended, we still acted from true partnership. Through empathic listening to one another and authentic communication, we were able to see that there was no future in continuing our romantic relationship. There was no blaming the other person that it didn't work out, no trying to control or change the other person to become what the other needed and wanted, and no conversation about who was right and who was wrong. By coming from true partnership we ended the relationship without significant upset or resentment. We were both sad that it had not worked, but the quality of the communication helped us move through the sadness faster and gave each of us a chance to learn something from the relationship.

The same can be true of relationships at work. There may be a time, as a manager, when it seems that you and one of your team members don't have a partnership. You are not working together toward the same goal, and you may reach a point where it is in the best interest of the company to let that person go. Even this "drastic" act can be handled from true partnership. Through straight communication and empathic listening, the people involved can go their separate ways with mutual respect and no resentment.

True partnership is a way you perceive the other person and a way you interact with the other person that does not invalidate their point of view, no matter what form the relationship may take, whether there is a partnership or not.

*How do I get others to try a true partnership perspective?*

There is nothing magical here. It is not about tips or strategies to get them to do it. Most people will not resist a shift to true partnership; it is natural for them to see the benefit. What they will resist is being pushed or coerced. There are three simple things that you can do: invite them to try it for themselves, share your enthusiasm, and walk the talk.

Perhaps the easiest thing to do is to invite them to try true partnership for themselves to determine if it is something they would like to have in their lives. An invitation can be as simple as this: "I just learned some new tools for building better relationships. Are you interested in hearing about them?" A simple invitation. If the other person does not accept your invitation, drop it. Most people don't want unsolicited advice about their relationships, and without acceptance of your invitation anything you say will probably come across as advice and be automatically discarded. A friend of mine recently read a great little book with some sound information about life. Her husband picked it up and was thumbing through it, and she said: "You should read that book, it would really help you." He immediately put it down and has shown no interest in it since. Her "you-message" had come across as unwarranted advice and criticism. It may have been more effective to make an invitation, such as "I really learned a lot from that book. Are you interested in hearing about it?"

If you saw a great movie over the weekend, it would be very natural to *share your enthusiasm* for the film with others. When we want to share our enthusiasm about something with others, we usually do four things. Using the movie example, we share our excitement about the movie, we explain what the movie was about, we say why we liked it, and we make a recommendation. Sharing your enthusiasm for true partnership is much the same process.

- *Share your excitement.* Say something like "Wow, I just finished a great book last week" or "I read a great book about true partnership that really had a major impact on me." Just be authentic and use I-language.
- *Explain what true partnership is about.* You might say that true partnership is about "How to be more effective in our relationships" or "How to operate more successfully at work" or "How to communicate so we can get more done through other people." Don't make it difficult or try to teach anything, just describe it in a simple sentence or two.
- *Say why you liked it.* Share a personal insight that you got out of applying the true partnership model. For example, you might say "I really saw how much my relationships are shaped by the assumptions and beliefs I bring to the table" or "I really saw how much I can improve my ability to listen to others." You can also share how the principles and practices of true partnership helped you improve a particular relationship. Above all, make it personal, be authentic, and be honest about what you got out of the true partnership approach.
- *Make a recommendation.* Don't be shy; use I-language. Say something like "I think you would really get a lot of value from this book." If you know the person well enough, you could say "I think you would get a lot from this book, especially in how to deal with that boss of yours." Whatever you decide, communicate what you think the value would be for the other person. Remember, your purpose is not to fix some-

thing that is wrong or to teach something that is right. True partnership is simply a tool that could possibly improve the relationships this person has at home and at work.

Enthusiasm is contagious. Sharing your enthusiasm about true partnership is one way to get others to try it for themselves.

Finally, perhaps the most powerful thing to do is to walk the talk. True partnership is a unique way of perceiving the world that is very noticeable to those around you. When you master the principles and practices of true partnership, you will see things that others don't see, you will discover solutions to problems that other people simply tolerate, and you will create connections to other people that make them feel very comfortable around you. Because most of us operate from the drift, people who operate from true partnership really stand out. Other people will notice and will naturally want what you have.

*What is the role of a leader in building an organization's culture of true partnership?*

When I hear this question, I am always concerned that the person who asks it is trying to abdicate his or her responsibility in creating a true partnership perspective. So let me first address that issue. Granted, an organization's culture has a great impact on individual behavior, so it is important to focus on creating a highly effective culture. Many organizations spend a great deal of time, effort, and money trying to change the culture, yet few succeed. What most of us forget is that individuals shape the culture. So there is a paradox that we must be aware of: To change the organizational culture that shapes individual thinking, we must focus on the individual. True partnership is an individual phenomenon, an individual decision. It does not matter what the culture of the organization is; individuals are still responsible for the effectiveness of their own relationships. The bottom line is that an organization is where people unite to accomplish some purpose. If you are more able to do your part to achieve these objectives by operating from a true partnership perspective, then your actions are consistent with the purpose.

Having addressed the issue of personal responsibility, let's look at the crux of the question. Even though I believe everyone has a role in creating the culture, it is true that people in leadership positions have greater influence because of their visibility and their decision-making power. By leadership positions, I am referring to those people in management and senior executive jobs. I believe the term *leader* can apply to a person at any level of an organization, but here I am addressing people in key senior positions.

If every one of us lights a candle, it will make for a brighter world, and I fundamentally agree. But I have been surprised at how easy it is for a leader to snuff out the candles in an organization. Intentionally or unintentionally, it happens. In my opinion, the role of a leader is to supply the oxygen to keep the flames burning.

True partnership represents a significant shift in people's thinking. This shift to true partnership cannot be forced on another, but there is much that leaders can do to help facilitate people's transition to this new perspective. Here are some things for leaders to consider to make true partnership available in their organization:

- Focus on the quality of relationships.
- Realize the limitations of the drift and the consequences to the organization.
- Create an opportunity for people to learn true partnership.

Let's examine each of these ideas in more detail.

*Focus on the quality of the relationships.*
First and foremost, leaders must recognize the importance of the internal and external relationships for organizational success. Leaders must establish the organizationwide expectation that relationships matter—that they are a priority. This focus should not, however, be at the expense of other factors for success. To prepare

a strong foundation for true partnership, leaders must see that boosting sales performance, effectively implementing new business strategies, enhancing customer loyalty, optimizing productivity, or improving profitability (or other means of measuring success) require a different quality of relatedness than what presently exists. For those of you who play golf, you know that to hit a golf ball farther you do not focus on hitting the ball farther—this is actually counterproductive. To hit a golf ball farther, you must relax and focus on the basics of a good swing. To do this is not to give up on the results. Likewise, if you focus on the quality of the internal and external relationships of an organization, you will end up improving the results, probably more than you might expect or predict. Most leaders do not know how results actually get produced, and they don't know that they don't know this. This leaves them in quite a predicament.

To consistently focus on financial results is counterproductive to improving financial performance for two reasons. One is that tearing apart a financial statement is simply an autopsy on what has already happened. The patient is already dead; nothing can be done to change the results. The second reason is that it takes the focus off what really matters in producing results—the effectiveness of the interactions between people. The quality of these interactions shape performance and results. The financial standards that are typically measured only report these results. Don't take your eye off these key benchmarks, but do keep them in perspective.

Do not take the quality of relationships for granted. Do not demean relationship enhancing skills as the "soft skills." Do not get swept up in the newest management fad and develop one new program after another to improve performance. Do not get swept away in the trendy thinking that technology will solve all the problems. Be sensitive to what you say and do because your actions have a much greater impact on the behavior of your team than you can imagine. Make it a personal and organizational priority to improve the way people relate to one another and go about producing results.

*Realize the limitations of the drift and the consequences to the organization.*

The drift, the traditional manner in which people relate to one another, has significant implications for every organization. The drift shapes how people interact with one another, the outcomes of those interactions, and what people see as possible and achievable. It sets up we–they thinking and inherent blaming that can cripple an organization's ability to operate effectively. It creates an atmosphere of power and control and subsequent game playing, resentment, and resignation. An organization operating from the drift wastes a great deal of time debating from a right–wrong posture. Additionally, when people in an organization operate from the drift, they see people, places, and events as "that's just the way he/she/it is" and feel a sense of helplessness in making a difference in the organization. Another "new" performance review system will be doomed to the same outcomes as its predecessors unless the context in which it is implemented is altered.

The practices of ineffective communicating and relating shaped by the drift are taken for granted, but they are simply too costly to ignore. Leaders have an opportunity to access the tremendous pool of human potential that lies untapped in most organizations, but they must first focus on the real obstacles to organizational performance.

*Create an opportunity for people to learn true partnership.*

Perhaps nothing is more important on a leader's list of priorities than creating this opportunity. This is not another item to check off. This is the foundation item that will influence every other item on the list. Do not think that "Either I have the time or budget to do this or to do item number four." A more appropriate way of thinking is that "I must get this done in order for my other projects to have a greater chance of succeeding."

A true partnership leader facilitates people's growth. Take the opportunity to examine the context that is shaping the relationships that influence the results produced. Have people look at how the drift shaped certain events and how true partnership might have allowed for different results. Make this examination a part of the organizational culture. Set aside some time at the end of each meeting to discuss the process, and even schedule occasional meetings to specifically address the quality of the relationships in your organization.

Perhaps most important of all, make the practice of dialogue a normal part of the organizational culture. Dialogue is a powerful tool that puts the principles and practices of true partnership into action. Use it and experience the rewards.

True partnership is a new set of principles and practices that people must learn. It is not a one-time training event. It must be woven into the very fabric of an organization. This will not happen without the personal dedication and commitment of leadership. Most important, you must develop a true partnership mind-set yourself and model it before you ask others to change.

Most leaders have no real idea of the impact that their behaviors have on their organization. A leader must walk the talk.

## Creating a World of True Partnership

A revolution in our approach to relating to one another evokes the capabilities that lie untapped within you and I as individuals, within our families, within our organizations, and within our world. We can only accomplish so much by ourselves. When we change the focus from a personal effectiveness model to an interpersonal effectiveness model, we realize the synergistic power of people living and working together. Through true partnership we can fulfill the opportunities available to us:

- As individuals we can discover the joy and satisfaction that comes from living and working effectively with others.

- Families can provide the structure of support parents and children need in facing today's circumstances and challenges.
- In our organizations we can develop new levels of teamwork and productivity to meet the challenges posed by the competitive and challenging global marketplace.
- As a society we can create breakthroughs in our ability to deal with the complex and difficult issues we face today and in the future.
- On an international level we can build relationships that foster peace, cooperation, and security in our world.

Ultimately, true partnership is about something more than individual and organizational effectiveness. It is about the future. It is what is necessary to create a sustainable world that will nurture future generations.

Artist Paul Gauguin once said that there are only two kinds of artists, plagiarists and revolutionaries. In my context, plagiarists are those who do relatively well or badly within the drift of the period. They are doing the best they can, considering the circumstances. Revolutionaries create an entirely new style—true partnership. They stick their necks out for something they believe enhances their world. Revolutionaries are the people who really generate change.

The drift is grounded in the principles of being separate and autonomous, of relating to others through power and control, and of either–or thinking. This fixed view of our world is simply too limiting and too costly. The consequences to us all if we continue down this same path are great. It is time to expose the myths and question the assumptions that shape our current relationships and our results.

The future depends on each of us raising the bar by committing ourselves to a new perspective of true partnership. We must each become a revolutionary and call on those around us to do the same. Only through a significant shift in our thinking can we transform the world we leave for our children and our children's children.

"Tomorrow we'll screw up our courage and cross the border. And you will see we will not fall off the edge of the world. We'll just find ourselves in new territory. In new territory never explored by anyone in your culture, because the maps say it isn't there" (Quinn 1992, 91).

You and I can have a significant impact on our individual effectiveness, our family harmony, the productivity of our organizations and institutions, the social issues our communities face, and the stability of our world by taking a stand for true partnership. You and I can create extraordinary relationships. New possibilities await us as we look beyond the horizon of our existing world and explore new territory. You and I can create the world anew.

# REFERENCES

Argyris, Chris. 1990. *Overcoming Organizational Defenses*. Boston: Simon and Schuster.

Blanton, Brad. 1995. *Radical Honesty—How to Transform Your Life by Telling the Truth*. New York: Dell.

Brian, Denis. 1996. *Einstein, A Life*. New York: John Wiley & Sons.

Bohm, David. 1990. "On Dialogue." Ojai, David Bohm Seminars.

———. 1980. *Wholeness and the Implicate Order*. New York: Routledge.

Capra, Fritjof. 1975. *The Tao of Physics*. Boston: New Science Library.

———. 1982. *The Turning Point—Science, Society, and the Rising Culture*. New York: Simon & Schuster.

———. 1996. *The Web of Life*. New York: Doubleday.

Einstein, Albert. 1988. *Albert Einstein: Philosopher-Scientist*. Edited by Paul Arthur Schlipp. New York: Open Court Publishing.

Eisler, Riane. 1987. *The Chalice and the Blade—Our History, Our Future*. New York: HarperCollins.

Ellinor, Linda, and Glenna Gerard. 1998. *Dialogue—Rediscover the Transforming Power of Conversation*. New York: John Wiley & Sons.

Gordon, Thomas. 1977. *Leader Effectiveness Training—The No-Lose Way to Release the Productive Potential of People*. New York: Wyden Books.

———. 1977. *Parent Effectiveness Training*. P.E.T. New York: Wyden Books.

Handy, Charles. 1998. *The Hungry Spirit—Beyond Capitalism: A Quest for Purpose in the Modern World*. New York: Broadway Books.

Harman, Willis. 1998. *Global Mind Change—The Promise of the 21st Century*. San Francisco: Berrett-Koehler.

Holmes, Joan. 1988. "Altering An Era." The Hunger Project Global Meeting, New York, New York.

Laing, R. D. 1970. *Knots*. New York: Pantheon Press.

Laszlo, Ervin. 1985. "The Crucial Epoch," *Futures*, February.

Maturana, Humberto, and Francisco Varela. 1992. *The Tree of Knowledge—The Biological Roots of Human Understanding*. Boston: Shambhala.

Montuori, Alphonso, and Isabella Conti. 1993. *From Power to Partnership—Creating the Future of Love, Work, and Community*. San Francisco: HarperCollins.

Poliner, Racheal A., and Jeffery Benson. 1997. *Dialogue: Turning Controversy into Community*. Boston: Educators for Social Responsibility.

Quinn, Daniel. 1992. *Ishmael—An Adventure of the Mind and Spirit*. New York: Bantam.

Rogers, Carl. 1980. *A Way of Being*. Boston: Houghton Mifflin.

Scieszka, Jon. 1989. *The True Story of the 3 Little Pigs! by A. Wolf*. New York: Puffin Books.

Stone, Doug, Bruce Patton, and Sheila Heen. 1999. *Difficult Conversations—How to Discuss What Matters Most*. New York: Penguin Books.

Wheatley, Margaret. 1992. *Leadership and the New Science—Learning about Organization from an Orderly Universe*. San Francisco: Berrett-Koehler.

Wheatley, Margaret, and Myron Kellner-Rogers. 1996. *A Simpler Way*. San Francisco: Berrett-Koehler.

Zaiss, Carl, and Thomas Gordon. 1993. *Sales Effectiveness Training—The Breakthrough Method to Become Partners with Your Customers.* New York: Dutton.

Zohar, Danah. 1990. *The Quantum Self—Human Nature and Consciousness Defined by the New Physics.* New York: William Morrow & Company.

Zohar, Danah, and Ian Marshall. 1994. *The Quantum Society—Mind, Physics, and a New Social Vision.* New York: William Morrow & Company.

# Index

# About the Author

FOR MORE THAN THIRTY YEARS CARL ZAISS has examined the question of what makes some individuals and some organizations more successful than others. His background includes sixteen years in the hotel industry in both property level and home office staff positions. His extensive experience in sales, marketing, operations, and general management led him to develop an innovative leadership style that fostered people development, a strong orientation toward customer needs, and increased productivity and satisfaction through teamwork.

In 1982 he founded Zaiss International to share his views on the importance of communication and relationships with a wider segment of the marketplace. Through his consulting, training, speaking, and writing, Carl continues his exploration of the issues of individual and organizational excellence.

Carl began to lead programs on relationships in the early 1980s. These early courses focused on the development of specific communication skills for sales and customer service personnel. His first book on the subject was *Sales Effectiveness Training*, co-authored with Dr. Thomas Gordon and published in 1993. This book is now available in paperback in seven languages.

In the early 1990s Carl shifted his focus to examining the power of context on individual and group behavior. During this period he developed and refined the new distinction of true partnership. He now consults, coaches, speaks, and trains people to apply the basic principles of true partnership. Because the fundamental principles of true partnership have such broad application and are relevant to so many areas, he works in the fields of sales, customer service, management, team effectiveness, and leadership development. His clients include Fortune 100 organizations, small entrepreneurial companies, and individuals.

Carl has raised four children, John, Scott, Kelly, and Brett, and has four grandchildren, Zac, Zoe, Jayna, and Olivia. He lives in Clifton, Virginia with his fiancée, Mickey.

For more information about the consulting, coaching, training, and speaking services that Carl provides, please contact:

Carl Zaiss
*Telephone* 800-239-4685
*Fax* 703-631-0427
*Email* carl@carlzaiss.com
or visit our Web site
www.carlzaiss.com

# Berrett-Koehler Publishers

BERRETT-KOEHLER is an independent publisher of books, periodicals, and other publications at the leading edge of new thinking and innovative practice on work, business, management, leadership, stewardship, career development, human resources, entrepreneurship, and global sustainability.

Since the company's founding in 1992, we have been committed to supporting the movement toward a more enlightened world of work by publishing books, periodicals, and other publications that help us to integrate our values with our work and work lives, and to create more humane and effective organizations.

We have chosen to focus on the areas of work, business, and organizations, because these are central elements in many people's lives today. Furthermore, the work world is going through tumultuous changes, from the decline of job security to the rise of new structures for organizing people and work. We believe that change is needed at all levels—individual, organizational, community, and global—and our publications address each of these levels.

We seek to create new lenses for understanding organizations, to legitimize topics that people care deeply about but that current business orthodoxy censors or considers secondary to bottom-line concerns, and to uncover new meaning, means, and ends for our work and work lives.

See next pages for other publications from Berrett-Koehler

### The New Why Teams Don't Work
### What Goes Wrong and How to Make it Right

Harvey Robbins and Michael Finley

Many teams run into trouble, say Harvey Robbins and Michael Finley, because teams themselves fail to think through the human implications of teaming. This practical guide teaches team members and team leaders how to maintain the highest level of team intelligence—providing the skills, attitudes, and emotional flexibility needed to get the most out of a team's inherent differences.

Paperback original, 270 pages • ISBN 1-57675-110-4
Item #51104-395 $17.95

### PeopleSmart
### Developing Your Interpersonal Intelligence

Mel Silberman, PhD, with Freda Hansburg, PhD

Everyone is in the people business, because all of us deal with other people all the time. That's why it's smart to reap the benefits of this eminently practical guide. *PeopleSmart* details the eight essential skills of interpersonal intelligence and provides a powerful plan for becoming more effective in every relationship—with supervisors, coworkers, a spouse, family, and friends.

Paperback original, 300 pages • ISBN 1-57675-091-4
Item #50914-395 $16.95

### The Influence Edge
### How to Persuade Others to
### Help You Achieve Your Goals

Alan A. Vengel

Alan Vengel teaches you the influence skills you need to enlist the cooperation of others, inside and outside the organization to achieve your professional goals. Drawing on case studies and illustrative anecdotes from his consulting practice, Vengel introduces a powerful system of influence initiatives and strategic thinking that anyone can apply to almost any work situation.

Paperback original, 114 pages • ISBN1-58376-156-X
Item #6156X-395 $15.95

**Berrett-Koehler Publishers**
PO Box 565, Williston, VT 05495-9900
Call toll-free! **800-929-2929** 7 am-12 midnight
Or fax your order to 802-864-7627
For fastest service order online: **www.bkconnection.com**

## Customers As Partners
### Building Relationships That Last

Chip R. Bell

Written with passion and humor, this groundbreaking work provides step-by-step guidelines for enhancing long-term customer loyalty and achieving lasting success. Chip Bell offers insights on how to keep the quality of customer relationships central in every interaction by creating sustaining personal bonds— the true source of a company's profitability.

Paperback, 256 pages, 1/96 • ISBN 1-881052-78-8
Item #52788-395 $15.95

Hardcover 9/94 • ISBN 1-881052-54-0 • Item #52540-395 $24.95

## Dance Lessons
### Six Steps to Great Partnerships in Business and Life

Chip R. Bell and Heather Shea

In this important guide, authors Chip Bell and Heather Shea offer an in-depth look at how we can successfully manage partnerships and build them with substance-passion, quality, heart, and soul. They show how we can successfully manage and build partnerships in all ares of our work and life.

Hardcover, 200 pages, 9/98 • ISBN 1-57675-043-4
Item #50434-395 $24.95

Audiotape, 2 cassettes/3 hrs. • ISBN 1-56511-272-5
Item #12725-395 $17.95

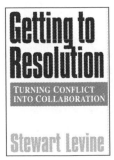

## Getting to Resolution
### Turning Conflict Into Collaboration

Stewart Levine

Stewart Levine gives readers an exciting new set of tools for resolving personal and business conflicts. Marriages run amuck, neighbors at odds with one another, business deals gone sour, and the pain and anger caused by corporate downsizing and layoffs are just a few of the conflicts he addresses.

Hardcover, 200 pages, 3/98 • ISBN 1-57675-005-1
Item #50051-395 $19.95

**Berrett-Koehler Publishers**
PO Box 565, Williston, VT 05495-9900
Call toll-free! **800-929-2929** 7 am-12 midnight
Or fax your order to 802-864-7627
For fastest service order online: **www.bkconnection.com**

# Spread the word!

**Berrett-Koehler books and audios are available at quantity discounts for orders of 10 or more copies.**

## True Partnership
### Revolutionary Thinking About Relating to Others
Carl Zaiss

MEDICAL LIBRARY
NORTH MEMORIAL HEALTH CARE
3300 OAKDALE AVENUE NORTH
ROBBINSDALE, MN 55422-2900

Paperback original, 150 pages
ISBN 1-57675-166-X
Item #5166X-395 $15.95

To find out about discounts on orders of 10 or more copies for individuals, corporations, institutions, and organizations, please call us toll-free at (800) 929-2929.

To find out about our discount programs for resellers, please contact our Special Sales department at (415) 288-0260; Fax: (415) 362-2512. Or email us at bkpub@bkpub.com.

**BK**

**Berrett-Koehler Publishers**
PO Box 565, Williston, VT 05495-9900
Call toll-free! **800-929-2929** 7 am-12 midnight
Or fax your order to 802-864-7627
For fastest service order online: **www.bkconnection.com**